ANGELS OF BANGKOK

INSIDE THE SECRET WORLD OF THAI

PROSTITUTION

G.T. GRAY

Published in 2012 by MAVERICK HOUSE
PUBLISHERS, Office 19, Dunboyne Business Park,
Dunboyne, Co. Meath, Ireland.

info@maverickhouse.com
http://www.maverickhouse.com

ISBN: 978-1-908518-09-5

5 4 3 2 1

The paper used in this book comes from wood pulp of
managed forests. For every tree felled, at least one tree is
planted, thereby renewing natural resources.

A CIP catalogue record for this book is available from the
British Library.

For the Angels, and all those who have shared their experience, strength and hope through the years

TABLE OF CONTENTS

ACKNOWLEDGEMENTS

The author would like to acknowledge the help of friends who offered encouragement and advice, including Gillian in Hoboken who told me I "had" to do this after hearing the idea. To Rob for his invaluable help in getting the project going, and BG, without whom it would never have been finished. I could never have been able to do this without the dedication of my translator Phapawee, who bridged many cultural gaps as well as translating. Also my brother Robert for his moral support, and the two Mikes in Pattaya. Finally, a big thanks to Maverick House for giving me a chance and to Fiona Lacey for her guidance and patience.

FOREWORD

It would be a wonderful world if we all came from homes with enough room for everyone, and two loving parents who had enough time and education to help us with our homework, who had money to send us to good schools, buy us books and computers. But the world isn't that way. People have to make the best lives they can for themselves with what they have available to them. For the women in this book, life is that way.

Most of these interviews were conducted over an 18-month period beginning in 2008. I hope some of these women have moved on, I found that tracking most of them was next to impossible. I don't know if the stories they tell are completely truthful. Like all of us, they probably exaggerate some aspects of their lives and downplay others.

Angels of Pattaya is not an apology for the way things are or a cry to sweep the bars and streets. This book was compiled because I thought the women should have a chance to tell their own stories. I found that listening to them talk about their own lives was illuminating. What struck me first was that the women don't want anyone to feel sorry for them: they just want people to understand why they do what they do. The women who were gracious enough to speak to me seemed to appreciate someone taking the time to listen. Almost without exception they thought the book was a good idea and wanted to have their stories heard, hoping it would bring a little understanding of them and the lives they lead.

Many of the women, despite having to drop out of school at anywhere from seven to 15 years of age, are bright and articulate. No matter how you may view these women, they have feelings about their lives and what they do.

Some are in the business out of desperation for money, others out of greed. Some see it as an easy lifestyle (sleeping until the afternoon, hanging out with friends all night – the act of being with a customer only takes up about an hour of the day). Some hold out a genuine hope of meeting a good man who will take them out of the hard life and into a better one. Many who get out of the life return – relationships are difficult. Language and cultural differences are many times insurmountable.

Interviews were conducted by providing the women with a list of questions written in Thai. Those who were willing to talk I met with a translator for interviews. Some spoke English well and were able to conduct the interview in English. Transcriptions were written in Thai-English; this is the way that the women spoke to me. Whenever possible, after translating the stories, the women were contacted to clear up any questions I had.

All of the women interviewed for this book are over 18. They have all made a choice (in most cases based on economic necessity) whether to be "in the business" or not.

All the women were paid for their time. I am grateful to them for their willingness to speak frankly about their chosen profession and the life that it entails.

BACKGROUND

While most people think of prostitution in Thailand in modern terms, it is helpful to understand it in the historical context. In 1905, the Slave Abolition Act ended all forms of slavery in Thailand. Prior to this a system of "bonded slavery" had existed in Thailand, whereupon a citizen could choose to sell him or herself into servitude to pay off a debt or to provide for the remaining family. The Sale of Wives by Husbands Act, which outlawed husbands who sold their wives without their consent, was enacted by King Rama IV in 1868. However, there remained three categories of women within the law. The law allowed men to buy women to become "third" wives, the lowest category of wives. The first category were legally wed wives; the second were women not legally wed to the men, but who bore their children (minor wives); and the third were, in simple terms, sex slaves. Following the Slave Abolition Act in 1905, as the slave wives disappeared, many of

13

the women who would have been third wives entered prostitution, as brothels were legal at the time.

Prostitution remained legal in Thailand, and in the 1930's prostitutes were registered so that they could receive medical care. In 1960, under pressure from the United Nations, Thailand passed the The Act to Deter Prostitution. Anyone who offered sex for sale would be fined and/or given a jail sentence (up to two months). But in 1966 the Thai government passed another law which allowed for the creation of entertainment establishments offering "special services". This law was introduced in large part to generate income from the large numbers of American servicemen stationed in Thailand and Vietnam. The law did not legalize prostitution, but allowed the government to look the other way.

Responding to the demands of their clientele, many Thai entrepreneurs transformed their coffee shops and bars into brothels. Go-go bars and "anything goes" establishments offering sex shows opened.

Word of American servicemen's "R & R" – military slang for rest and recuperation (or rest and relaxation), is a term used for the free time of a soldier in the U.S. military – ventures in Bangkok and Pattaya gradually spread, and as the Vietnam War wound down and ended tourists began to frequent Thailand and the bar scene. Thailand's reputation for cheap and easy sex became as much a part of its lore as its temples and beaches.

How many prostitutes are there in Thailand? Estimates vary from the Government Health Department's number of 75,000 to some Non-Government Organization's (NGO's) estimates of up to two million. Both numbers are hard to imagine. For the NGO's number to be accurate we must believe 9% of Thai women between the ages of 18 to 49 are prostitutes. (Thailand's total population is approximately 64 million. The adult age group of 18 to 49 accounts for approximately 70% of the total population, and using 50% as the number of women, rounding off numbers, that gives us around 22,500,000 women in that age group). A more realistic estimate of women involved in the sex industry would probably be 400,000 to 500,000.

If you are moved by any of the stories in this book and want to do something about it, an organization of former sex-workers, called The Empower Foundation, could use your help. Visit **www.empowerfoundation. org** and ask how you can assist them.

"Over the last two decades more than 30,000 sex

workers have studied with Empower. For some of us it has been the first time we have been able to access our right to study. For others of us who finished school or university, we have gained new skills, knowledge and friendship."

– The Empower Foundation website.

1

Goy and Su: "We are real, not video"

Goy and Su are friends who work at a Bangkok massage parlour. It's one of the "fish-bowl" parlours, where the women sit behind a glass partition while the customers sit in a bar area and look them over before making a selection. This one caters to western and Indian customers; there are others around Bangkok that cater for Japanese, Korean and Thai men. A massage here costs 1,500 baht, of which the women get 500. Tips are optional. They were interviewed in a restaurant before starting their 5:00pm to 2:00am shift. Both were wearing heavy make-up, miniskirts and high-heeled shoes. There is no mistaking they are working girls. Goy is short, just over five feet tall, with dark skin, long straight black hair and big round eyes; without the make-up she would almost look Polynesian. Su is taller, and a bit heavier. Her hair is long and wavy.

Q: How old are you?

Goy: I am 22 years old.

Su: Me, I am 19 years old.

How long have you been working at this massage parlour?

Goy: I have been here for one year.

Su: Only two months.

Where do you come from?

Goy: I come from Isaan.

Su: I was born in Bangkok. I live here all my life.

What did you do for work before working here?

Goy: I was maid in condo. Job was okay, but not make enough money to send home to family. Salary only 4,000 baht every month. Pay for room, for food, clothes, nothing to give for family and daughter.

Su: I take care my baby. She is three year old; she stay with my mother while I work.

Goy, How old is your daughter?

Goy: She is four year old. She stay in Isaan with my mother and father. Yes, I miss her very much. I see her maybe one time in two month. I can go home for two or three day then.

So how many days a month do you work?

Goy: I work everyday. No work, no money.

Su: If I make good money in one week, maybe I not come for one or two day. But *Mamasan* not like a girl to not come and work. If customer come in and ask for girl, and she not working, maybe customer go home.

Goy: And it good for business to have many girls here everyday.

How much money do you make in one month?

Goy: For massage customer pay 1,500 baht. Girl get 500. Customer pay tip, sometimes 500 baht, sometimes 1,000, sometimes 2,000. Sometimes tip nothing. I can make maybe 10,000 baht, 15,000 for good month, good tip. One time a customer tip me 200 US dollars.

Su: First month I make about 10,000 baht. This month I think I make more. Have customer come back to see me. I give 3,000 baht to my family. Cannot give more. They think I work restaurant.

Goy: I send 5,000 baht to my family every month.

How did you start to work here?

Goy: I have a friend work here, she tell me I can make more money. I was afraid at first. Never go with *farang* man before.

Su: I have friend work at massage parlour on Ratchada Road (*an area with many massage parlours, mostly catering to Thai and Chinese clientele*). But I cannot work there, my skin too dark. So she tell me maybe I can work here at this place. More foreign men, like dark skin.

Why do you think western men like your dark skin and Asian men do not?

Goy: Not sure why *farang* man like us. They like small girl with dark skin. Maybe different from *farang* lady? They always say "my wife fat" or "my wife old". Thai man and Chinese man like *pew kow*. They say dark skin is ugly, for farm girls. So we cannot work in place for Thai and Chinese man.

Su: All Thai ladies want white skin. We think it is beautiful. Like on TV.

What do you think about the customers?

Goy: They come for good time. Have sex with girl. If they have good heart, okay, I like. But sometime they smell, are dirty. No good. First time I work, customer take me out, buy me clothes, jewellery. Stay at nice hotel. (*Laughing*) I think "this very good job." I never see him again. I remember him many times. I think, "Does he think about me, does he think good or bad?"

Su: I don't think too much about customer. They are customer. Some come back and are good men. Good tip, fun.

Do you ever like having sex with them?

Goy: (*Laughing*) Oh yes. Sometimes. If they make love slowly, not push me around. I am small, yes? So I don't like fat big man. But yes, sometimes feels good.

Su: I like some customer for sex. Same – if he go slowly, smile, say nice things, okay. If he let me do what I want for making love, I can like it, too.

20

Do you worry about AIDS and other disease?

Su: YES! I always tell customer use condom. I will not make love if him not use. Some man say give me more money, but I say no, must use. If not want, then only *chock-wow* (*use hand*).

Goy: I want man to use condom. I afraid [of] AIDS. Owner tell girl have to go to hospital for test blood. If have problem here (*points to crotch*) cannot work. Must stay home until finish.

What if you don't want to go with a customer?

Goy: We cannot see customer. They look at us in window, we cannot see them. But if we come out and see and we not want to go, we can say "sorry, not feel good, maybe better you pick different girl." But then Mamasan cut money for (*from*) next customer.

Su: Better to go with and try to finish man soon.

Do you like the job?

Goy: Sometimes, yes. Meet many men from different country. Learn many things. Learn to speak English. But we have to work hard. Job is to make man feel good. Sometimes make love to three, four men in one day. And give massage.

Su: I think it is okay. I want money, so work no problem. For money, good. Sometimes if no customer, boring. Sit, watch TV, talk with girls.

Do the girls like each other, or have problems?

Su: I never have problem with other girl. Only one time, yes, customer want to take two girls, I not want to go. I can go with two girls but I not want to with that customer. Other girl get angry me. But we talk, okay, now no problem.

Goy: We are okay together. But sometimes have a problem. If a girl spy for owner.

How do they spy for the owner?

Goy: Sometimes customer want to take girl outside. Meet after finish work. If owner find out, have big problem. Sometimes customer say "here phone number or room hotel, come see me." If a girl see another girl outside with man, maybe have problem.

You two are good friends, right? Did you know each other before?

Goy: No, I not know her before. We like each other. Sit, talk, laugh together.

Su: Yes, we have good time together working. She help me when I come to work first time. Tell me not to believe customer. Lie too much. Lie about "no, I no have girlfriend" [or] "Oh, darling I think about you all the time, I come back see you everyday."

Where do you live, who do you live with? Can you tell me about your room or house?

Goy: I live in a small room, near the northern bus station. I live alone, but have small room, only bed. No shower or toilet, that is outside, share with everyone. I pay 1,500 baht every month. In Isaan have a house with buffalo, chicken. I like house there. But there is no work, so I have to live here. I do not like Bangkok, but it is good for money.

Su: I live in Pratunam neighbourhood in Bangkok with my mother and father, my daughter and my young brother. It is a small house; I sleep with my daughter when I come home. Before [I get home] she sleeps with my mother and father. My brother sleep in big room (*main room of the house*). He go to school, he is 15 year old.

Have either of you ever been married, and do you have a husband or boyfriend now?

Su: I have husband before, but now divorce. We always fighting. He run around, drinking, gambling.

How long were you married?

Su: I don't know, maybe three year I think. I think he will be good father of my daughter. No, father of baby is different man. I have baby when I am 16. I stop going to school to have baby. Now, no boyfriend. Thai man I don't want, they don't want girl to work like this, but want money so they can run around. *Farang*, maybe sometime, if he is good man and take care me and baby.

Goy: I have no boyfriend. I am divorce from my husband, now almost three year. We marry when I am fifteen.

Did you leave school?

Goy: No, I not go to school. I work in restaurant with my mother.

When did you stop going to school?

Goy: When I am very young, maybe seven years old. Have to work to help my family.

You stopped going to school when you were seven years old? How is your reading and writing? I am sorry to ask, but in the West it is illegal for children not to attend school.

Goy: My reading is okay. My writing not too good. But better now. Maybe sometime I can go to school again. But for now, I am okay. But I cannot get a good job, I know.

What do you want to be doing in five or ten years time?

Goy: I want my own house in Isaan, and a shop, so I can take care of my daughter. Yes, I want a husband too. I think to stay alone no good.

How is it no good?

Goy: Who will take care when sick? What about when old? And will be lonely.

Su: I want a small house for me and baby, and a shop to sell things, so I don't have to work like this anymore.

What about a book about the women of Bangkok – do you think it's a good idea?

Goy: Yes, it is good idea, I think.

Su: Not sure. Maybe if *farang* read the book, I don't know. But I don't want some Thai girl to read and think we have good job.

What do you want to say about your life to the people who might read the book?

Goy: This life is hard, not easy. People think we are lazy, but we work for our family. No one can take care but us.

Su: Yes, we work. And *farang* not understand our life here. We want to have man treat us nice. We are not same as a movie, we are real, not video.

UPDATE: Six months after the initial interview, Goy and Su have moved on together to an upscale bar, which charges 3,500 baht for 90 minutes with a girl. The girls get half the fee, plus whatever tip the customer gives. The bar has private rooms upstairs to entertain customers (including having sex). They now see just one customer per night, work 26 days a month, and make an average of 50,000 baht per month (three times what the average office worker makes, almost ten times what a factory worker makes). They both have new mobile phones, and are dressed in clothes befitting office workers on a day off, or casual college students.

I asked them what they thought of their new situation:

Goy: It is much better here. Boss is nice to the girls, if we are tired we can go home, if we are sick we can call to him and say cannot work. It is no problem.

Su: The customers are better. More money (*laughing*). Oh yes, we have man come here this week and go with me and Goy together. After he tip $100 U.S.! One to me and one to Goy. I am happy here. Soon I will not have to work anymore. I have money in my bank. I can take care my daughter.

Goy: Yes, me too. My daughter she will go to school, and I will go home and be her mother again (*at this point she begins to cry a little*). She will not have a life the same as me. That is what I want. I am sorry I cry. I never talk like this before (*Su also starts to cry a little and holds Goy's hand*).

Su: I help my mother and father and my brother. Sometimes I do not like what I do to work, but I can take care my family and I am happy.

How much longer do you think you will work like this?

Goy: (*Still crying a little*) Maybe three months, maybe six months. I hope it is three. I want to go home and leave Bangkok. I never want to come here again.

Su: (*To Goy, laughing*) You have to come to see me, I am your sister now. I stop when Goy goes home. I cannot be here without Goy. I will be alone too much.

What would you say to a girl who was thinking of working or just starting to work as a prostitute?

Goy: If a girl cannot work another job and must take care of her baby or her parents, okay. But some girls think to work like this is fun. Meet foreign man and make money for go out to disco. Okay, but I think they will not be happy if they work like this for a long time. It is better to do some other job. Because maybe they will take drugs and drink too much so they can work like this. For many girls I see that happen. You must have a good friend to talk with and help you. Because it is lonely. And sad.

Su: If this the work they have to do, okay, it is their life. But I think they should know many times it is not a good life. I have been working for only about one year. Many times I am very sad. Yes, it is a sad life sometime. For us we have a hard life.

2

FON: "NOTHING MAKE ME SAD, NOTHING MAKE ME CRY NO MORE."

I met Fon at a restaurant across from the beer bar she works in as a free-lance bar girl. She and her friends sit at the bar waiting to meet a customer. Sometimes they meet a customer within five minutes, sometimes they go home without finding one. On the day that I meet her, there is no mistaking what Fon does for a living. She is wearing a short, tight mini-dress and spiked heels. She is wearing too much make-up and has shoulder length hair died a pale orange. She is tall and thin, and seldom smiles.

Q: Hello Fon, I am writing a book about the women who work in the bars of Thailand. Can you tell me a little about yourself – how old you are, where you are from, about your family?

Fon: Yes, I can tell you I am 29 year old. I come from Bangkok. You know Klong Toei? (*a slum neighbourhood in Bangkok, notorious for drugs and guns*) I born there. I now live there. I have one brother and one sister, they younger than me. I not see them for many year. I think my brother in the jail. My sister is good person, good in school, very smart. Now she have a job in some company about import and export. She good in school, good in life. My parent are…they have a problem. Many problem in their life. My father drink too much whiskey. Drunk many time, I remember he hit my mother, I cry, she cry, he hit and throw something. I am about six or seven year old, he leave. I think go some other place in Bangkok. He want to come back many time, my mother not want him. My mother take care me, my sister and my brother. To do this she work maid for company (*a cleaning service*). She work everyday and night, too. We not see her because she work too much.

So you took care of yourselves?

Yes. And then my mother she work so hard and she start to take drug – yaba – because she work too much. After her life and our life not good because we not have a mother. She work and take drug. (*Shrugs*)

Did you know that she was taking drugs?

Not know for long time. But we know she different, not the same before. And I stop to go to school when I am about 15. I get boyfriend and I have baby girl, when I am 15.

29

And what did your mother say?

She is sad I stop school but happy have a girl. And happy I can leave Klong Toei.

You moved away? How did your life go from there?

Yes, I stay with my boyfriend and his family. They live near our room, but not in Klong Toei. Have a nice house, big. My home is Klong Toei is one room. Yes, for everybody. With boyfriend family I think everything okay, but then something happen. We are together about three year. And my boyfriend his family not like me anymore. They say I must leave but my daughter will stay with them. Why they say this I don't know. Maybe because I come from Klong Toei, maybe because my mother take drug, I do not know. My boyfriend he not talk to me. They tell me to leave. My daughter she is about three year old. I am 18.

So you just had to leave their house? Why didn't you go to someone to help you?

They (*Fon's inlaws*) tell me I can see my daughter, but cannot live with them. I ask what is problem, they never say to me. Who can help me? I am poor girl from Klong Toei. His family more important than me. Police not listen me, no one listen me, no one care. So I go away and wait to see daughter again. But they lie and I not see her again.

You never saw her again, even now?

No. Last time I see her more than ten year ago.

That must be very difficult for you...

That time, yes. Now, no. It like everything now. Nothing make me sad, nothing make me cry no more.

Can you explain more about that?

How? I lose my daughter. My mother she die already. My brother in jail, I not see my father for so many year. Only my sister has good life, but I do not see her for about five year, she not like what I do and not talk with me any more. So in my life many thing happen no good. I not know why. I am not a bad person. If I cry I cry everyday. So I stop, now nothing make me cry again. And my heart turn hard.

What happened to you after you left your husband's family?

I come back Klong Toei, but stay with friend. Have about four or five friend stay together. One friend she tell me can go to Sukhumvit Road and find the westerner to have sex, can get money 500, 600 baht every time. She can go with two, three men every night. So I go with her.

What did you think about going out to have sex for money?

I don't care. I lose what is important to me, my daughter. What can happen I feel more bad than that?

And I think maybe if I can have some money and nice room I can have my daughter again. But not happen.

And what has happened over the past ten, eleven years?

I work Sukhumvit until 20 year old. Then I go to bar beer, work one, two year. I dancing in go-go bar some time, but I don't like. Go work bar beer in Phuket, Pattaya. Now I stay Bangkok again.

Have you had more children or a boyfriend or husband?

No more children for me. Only my daughter. I have boyfriend every night (*Fon laughs – the only time during the interview*). I never get marry again, but I have some boyfriend. One come from England I think, one from America. I have one Japan man send me money, I think he take me Japan. He good man, young man. But his family tell him cannot come back to Thailand, he call me and tell me he sorry but family want him to stay Japan, must do what parent say. So I not see him again.

Did his family know about you?

Yes, he say they not want him to be with Thai lady, only Japan. And we finish.

And what did you think about him?

He was nice boy. Now he gone, so I not think about him.

And the other boyfriends?

Say many thing like "I love you", "I come back for you". Lie. Now I don't know them.

So what do you think of your customers in general?

(*Shrugs*) Some are nice. But they are only customer. Why do I think they buy sex? I not know. I not care. Only care they come to me and pay me.

And how much do they pay you? How much do you make in one month?

Now. Customer must pay 1,500 baht for short-time. Long time 3,000 baht. I can make about more than 25,000 baht in one month.

So now you are working out of (*named*) beer garden, right? Do you go anywhere else? Do you work every night?

(*Shrugs again*) Up to me. I only come beer garden and wait for customer. Sometime come afternoon. Sometime come evening. If have customer in afternoon, maybe go home, maybe come back Beer Garden. Sometime if have money go another beer garden with friend, look for customer. Maybe go disco, if have money. If have money can work or not work. Up to me.

Do you ever think of doing something else? Your English is pretty good.

No, no different job for me to do. I don't want to work factory or cashier. Why not? Not money enough. So I go with man.

Do you ever hope or think you will see your daughter again?

No, I think I will never see her again. My husband family go somewhere, move near to Bangkok many year ago, but I do not know where. And now I am lady from the bar – what can I say to her? I think "do she think about me?" I always miss her, miss her forever.

Do you have friends you spend time with, other girls from the bar?

Yes, sure. We talk, go to shopping at market, many thing.

What do you talk about? Work, customers?

We talk about many thing. Some girl talk about the customer, me I do not. Why not? I not think, not care about customer. Maybe talk about money someone pay me sometime. If someone know some customer pay a lot of money maybe she will tell.

And the sex, do you like it, not like it?

(*Shrugs again*) I not like. For me it is work. But I not feel good or bad. Sometime I like to talk in bar to customer. Talk about their life. Sometime interesting. Say something funny.

What about HIV? Do you always use a condom?

Yes, customer must use condom. For young guy is no problem, they say "okay". Old man not want, but must use. I not want to get sick, die.

So you have been doing this for ten years. How many years do you think you will work? Do you have any plan or dreams for the future – five, ten years from now?

No, my dream stop many year ago. Before I think I work like this only a short time, but now is more than ten year already. Now I do not know if I work like this until I am old. Maybe sometime I will have money to open some shop like beauty shop or mini-store.

Okay, thank you for talking with me, Fon. What do you think of a book about the women who work in the bars? Is there anything you want to say to people who will read it?

Many girl here have a hard life. Not want to talk about this life. Me? No, I do not like to talk about it. It make me think about many thing I not want to think about. I do not like to talk about my life because I not understand why if I am good person I cannot have a good life. No one can tell me that. Can you?

3

Nu: "I think many men lonely"

Nu met me at a bar down the street from where she works in the city of Pattaya – famous for its number of bars, discos and available women. She is 22, just over 5' tall and says she weighs about 80 pounds, with long black hair that is tied back in a pony tail. Nu doesn't look like an exotic dancer, wearing a baggy t-shirt and "camo" shorts with sandals. But she has been dancing at three or four different go-go bars over the past year.

Nu, can you tell me where you come from?

Nu: I come from Nakhon Si Thammarat, in the south of Thailand. My parents not live in city, they live about 20 kilometres outside.

What do they do?

They have a small shop to sell part for car and truck. My father can fix car, truck, motorcycle also. My brother work there. But they don't make any money anymore, so two year ago I go to Bangkok in Samut Sakon (*small*

36

industrial town outside of Bangkok) to work in factory with my aunt. I make a food from fish.

Why didn't you just stay at that job?

Oh my God! The smell is so bad! (*Laughing*). Everyday I go home and smell like a fish. Everything. Hair, clothes. Always smell like a fish. And make so little money. 6,000 baht for one month.

And how did you end up in Pattaya?

One girl at the factory her sister work here in bar. Make money about 30,000 baht in one month. So I ask what she have to do. Her sister (*at the factory*) give phone number to me and I call to girl here. She tell me she dance at the go-go bar. I ask her about what she have to do – sleep with man? She tell me, sure, but money is nice, so it no problem, if not want to go with man, not go. If go, get 1,500 baht for one night, maybe can get more if tourist who is rich. So, I like to dance, I come to visit Pattaya, go to go-go bar. I think it is okay. Wear bikini, dance, drink with customer. So I say yes.

What did you tell your aunt, does she know?

(*Laughing*) No no no! I tell her I go to work cashier restaurant. Does she believe? I don't know. She say okay, my parents say okay. So I start dancing at go-go about one year ago.

And what did you think about it when you started?

It was no problem. Wear bikini, dance, listen to music. Other girls are nice to me. Customer seem like nice man. I don't go with man for about one month, then Ma (*Mamasan*) tell me I must go with the man.

Why didn't you go at first?

Not want to. I make money about 15,000 baht from salary and drinks and tip. Money enough (*laughing*). Was I virgin? (*Laughing again*) No! But I never go with *farang* before so I worry a little bit. About what? Don't know – (laughing) but other girls tell me "oh *farang* so big, not like Thai man." Is that true? (*Continues laughing*) Yes!

So what do you think now about the work after one year? You said you have worked at several bars, why?

I change bar because first bar many girl take drug. I do not take a drug. Many girl there take yaba or another drug so I leave that bar. Another bar I go to I must dance nude. No problem. After one night it is same as bikini dance. Not think about to be nude, just dance. But at that bar the owner try to cheat the girl. Take money if not get enough customer to buy drink or pay bar. He tell me salary one month 11,000 baht for nude dance. But when he pay me first time, he say "Oh, you have customer pay bar only four time, lady drink not enough, late two time, must cut salary." So I

38

get salary less than 9,000 baht and get new job at new bar. I dance there now more than seven month. It is okay. Good salary and tip. Nice customer. But now I am boring (*bored*) with job. Maybe not job, but boring (*bored*) with my life. In the future what can I do? If I dancing and go with man for how many year? What can I do when I am old lady? I think serious about this. So now I try to save my money, help my family. I hope in one year or two year I can go home and open a shop in my home. What shop? Maybe beauty shop or like a 7-Eleven. I think in two year I can have about 100,000 baht to bring home.

I don't mind to go with the man. If he is clean and not angry or drunk, sure it is not problem. Can go out to disco, food, maybe go to island or other beach to ride banana boat, shopping to Bangkok. I think many men lonely. Sex with man is short time, understand? About 30 minutes. But if man take me for long time like two days or more, then they want a girl to talk with them and be nice. That is okay, I can do that.

What if you met a nice foreign man, would you marry him or go abroad?

(*Nu thinks about this for a long minute*) I don't know. He would have to be rich (*shrugs her shoulders*). My family would not like it for me to marry a foreign man, but if he would take care of them they would say okay I think. I don't want to leave Thailand. I don't think I will like some other country. I would miss Thai people. And some other country is very cold, right? UK, German, Sweden. I see the picture of snow!

Some people would say that dancing nude in a bar and having sex with strange men is not a good job, that it is bad for a woman to do this job. What do you think?

I think people can think that. I know what people think about a bar girl. But they don't know. What if they lose the good job? Or have some mother or father get sick and need to make money more? So they can think what they think, but I don't think it's good they talk about a girl like that. Maybe they have to do this one day! I don't like to talk bad about someone, even customer. I don't like someone to talk bad about the bar girl – we only try to help our family.

You haven't mentioned children – do you have any?

No, no children. When I finish bar I will get married and have children, make sure they have a good life. That they can go to school and are happy.

Thank you Nu, is there anything else you want to say to

the people who will read this book?

Come to Thailand, enjoy. If come to Pattaya be nice to ladies, we want to have good time like you, but this is our job, and we have family we must take care [of].

4

PHEN: "I LIKE MONEY"

I interviewed Phen at the Bangkok bar where she works. The bar isn't open for another two hours, but the girls are sitting around watching a Korean movie dubbed into Thai on the television. The bar is a "beer bar", with no entertainment other than drinking, watching TV, and talking with the women. If a customer wants to take a woman out of the bar, the "bar fine" is 500 baht, of which the girls get 100 baht for the first ten fines each month, and 250 for every one after that. Phen charges customers 1,500 baht for a "short time", and 2,500 or 3,000 for all night. Phen is small, slim and has short hair, parted on the side and slicked down with gel. The haircut sets her apart from the other girls in the bar. She hasn't yet changed into her "uniform" – either a short dress or miniskirt – and hasn't put on her make-up. In her sandals, jeans and black sleeveless turtleneck, she looks like a 60's co-ed. You do notice her gold right away – it's worn as fashion, and also a sign of pride and status by many bar girls. She has a gold chain around her neck, with a gold amulet attached. She has gold bracelets on each wrist and also has a gold chain around one ankle.

Q: Hi Phen, can you tell me a little about yourself – how old are you, how did you start working here?

Phen: I am 20 year old. I work in this bar since I am 18 year old. What else can I do? I have a baby when I am 16. I get pregnant when I am 15. I meet a Thai man. He already have a wife, I know that, but I am young and stupid. He tell me he give money for the baby, but that is a lie. My mama and papa ask him for money after I have the baby, and he tell them "No, I cannot." His family is important, and he tell my parents if they make trouble, they will have some problem. I have to leave school, I cannot get job anywhere. I have to leave my baby two year ago with [my] mama and come here for work.

How did you know to come to Bangkok and go to work in a bar?

I know girls from the village who come to Bangkok. Everyone in the village know a girl who come here.

What do people in the village think of girls who come

here to work?

They know what us girls do here, some people think bad about it. But if their daughter or son (laughing), have to do it – their daughter or son send 5,000 baht every month it is not so bad to them.

What about working here – what do you think about it?

About my work? I like money. You see, I have gold for my neck, wrists and ankles. I have money in the bank, too. How much? (*Laughing*) More than anyone back in my home. Sometime I look at the girls who sell some things on the street – food or fruit or lottery. I am from Isaan – the same as them – you can know we are because the skin, it is *pew-dam*. We cannot get good jobs, we are only poor farm girls; the only thing they can do is sell noodles or somtam (spicy Thai papaya salad). You look how people – Thai people – work in the office: look at them. They do not respect them. Would I be happy to make noodles for someone who does not respect me? For how much? 200 baht for one day? I think I could not do that. When I go home to the village now, I have money to give Mama, my sister and my baby. That make me happy.

What else does money buy?

I can go to shopping with my friends. Or to dancing

or to buy something special for my baby. And for the bank.

How much money do you make?

In the bar I can make 2,000 or 3,000 baht in one night. Customers take me to Phuket and Pattaya, stay in nice hotels, sleep late, go for trip to island.

But do you make that much every night? There must be nights when you don't have a customer. How much do you make in one month?

(*With a smirk*) No, I have a lot of customer. In one month, maybe I can make 40,000, 50,000 baht. Yes, sometimes, no customer. But I think I am smart here – I know the customer – if he will go with me or only want to talk.

How do you know that?

Not sure, but I look everything in the man – I look his face, what he drink, if he buy me drink, if he look other lady while he talk to me. Maybe he do not want me to touch him. Many things.

What do you think of the men who come to the bar?

Some men are nice, and we want to know "why do you come here, why you not have a girl at home in Australia or Germany or England?" Why they not want to meet one girl and stay with her? Why man always want to [be a] playboy? But if a man is nice, treat girl

45

nice, like to have a good time, okay, no problem, I will have fun with a man like that.

How about working with the other girls, are you all friends?

Yes, the girls are my friends. We understand each other. I like to be friends with all other girls. We joke about our life, joke about the customer. If a girl have a problem we listen. If one has a broken heart, we all cry. Me? I will never have broken heart again. Before yes, but not now. Too many men lie, how can I believe? They say "oh, I write to you, I come back for you, I miss you." I don't believe from a long time ago. I tell them [to] send money.

Do they send money?

Sometimes they send money and letter, or e-mail, say nice things. Sometimes I don't remember the face, or what they look like, you know? So if a man come in the bar and say "Hello sweetheart, I miss you", I don't know if they joking or not. I don't know if they come in last week or last year. But I say "oh, *tee-lock* (*sweetheart*), I miss you too" and kiss big. And I ask question "how is your life? How is your job?" [I] Try to remember who he is (*laughing*).

How long do you think you will work in the bars?

Not sure, maybe someday I will have enough money

to stop working, I hope before I get too old (*laughing*). How much is money enough? Never enough, but maybe I will meet a rich man and will give me enough to stop working.

Do you have a boyfriend?

Now, my life is okay. I do not need boyfriend. Thai men only want money. Foreign man only want sex.

Are you ever lonely?

Sometimes I am lonely, I miss my baby always. But I have friends.

Do you live alone?

I live with two girls, they work in another bar, right over there (*pointing across the walkway*). We have apartment, we pay 5,000 baht every month. It is nice. We have one bedroom and another room. We have TV, *tu-yen* (*refrigerator*), sofa, tables. Not like when I first come here to Bangkok and live up there (*points above the bar*) and share a little room with only a bed with two more girl.

Would you ever bring a customer to your room?

No, I would never bring a man to my room. It is ours. For us only.

Are you happy in your life?

I am happy I can take care [of my] baby and family. I not worry about myself. I like to buy nice things –

clothes, cosmetic, gold. It make me happy. So to be happy I must do this job.

Is there anything else you want to tell people about you and your friends, your lives?

We do what we do. If you are nice, we are nice. But we have sex different man everyday. We try to have many so we make more money. I know I'm thinking sometimes a man think we are like, what, the fish that eats everything. Shark? So, how would you be if this was your job?

5

Buey: "I don't feel good, I don't feel bad"

I met Buey at a Thai fast-food restaurant, half a block away from the corner she stands on almost every night. The corner is a bus stop on one of Bangkok's main streets, but doubles as a hang-out for working girls. If the police ever do decide to ask them what they are doing, the answer is "waiting for the bus". Buey is tall, a bit heavy, and with her make-up and shortie t-shirt, baggy jeans and black high top sneakers she could be an LA gangster girl. At first glance she looks a lot younger than 27, but from under the make-up the lines of a hard life show through.

Q: Hi Buey, tell me about yourself – where you are from, how old you are, your life today, what you would like for the future.

Buey: I come from Buriram in the northeast of Thailand. I am 27 year. Now I am a girl who work here on the *soi*, waiting for man.

You are from Buriram. How long have you been in Bangkok, why did you come here?

I come here to earn money to take care of my family. In my family are many people, my two sons who stay with my mother, my grandmother and grandfather. I also have two brothers, but they are no good. And I have sister work at massage near to here.

You said your brothers are no good, why not?

My father die when we are young. I am six, my sister five, my brothers very young, maybe one or two and three year old. So my mother and grandmother and grandfather must take care us. I cannot go to school after I am about 12 year old. I must work. What I do? I work in restaurant my grandmother have. My grandfather is farmer. My younger sister go to school until she is same – about 12 year old. Then she help work in restaurant. My brothers can go to school, but when they are, what you say, teenager, they start to be bad boys. Steal motorcycle, some other things. Have a lot of trouble for my mother. So the police take them away, maybe [for] one year. They come back and [are] sometime good, sometime bad. But their friends always bad and they start to take drug. Now they stay [in] prison because they take money from some shop. Two year already. Must stay more, maybe two or three year,

I don't know. So they do not help my family. I come to Bangkok about more than three year ago. Before in Buriram I have Thai guy stay with me. He is father of my sons. But he now stay with another girl. Because he like to drink and he hit me and sons. So my grandfather go to kill him one day. He run away (*laughing*) and never come back. My grandfather tell me he say he is sorry, but I think nevermind. I think this is better for my sons.

So did you come here to work like this or did you do something else first?

I find job, work in office near to here, work was maid. I am maid for about two year, then stop work because company say [they] have too many maid and I stop.

What was your salary for being a maid?

My salary about 5,500 baht for one month.

And how did you start doing this?

I was maid at night. I walk around here, I see many *farang* and many lady. Sometime at night *farang* (*foreigner*) say something to me. I talk with other lady who are maid. One girl she say she go with *farang* sometime and give her 800 or 1,000 baht for sex. So when job finish I just walk around one night and meet *farang* guy over there (*pointing to a coffee shop*). He ask me can I go with him and I say okay I ask him how much he give me he say have 1,000 baht but must pay for short-time hotel about 180 baht, so I can have 800 baht. I say "okay". That [was] about two year ago. (*Laughing*) I still see that guy sometime.

So, do you work in a bar?

No, I work over there – waiting for bus (*laughing*).

And do you meet a man every night?

Not now. But [during] tourist time I can.

And how much do you charge for sex?

1,000 baht. But if man say [he] can give 700 baht and [I] have no customer, I say okay.

And how much do you make in one week or one month?

Depend on man. How many. Sometime I can get two or three men one night, then I wait for two or three day, come back. In a month I can get about 15,000 baht or more.

Do you think this is dangerous? What about AIDS?

About AID, man use condom or [I do] not go. Yes always. [I do] not want to die. I have two son to think about. I must take care for them.

And what do you think about the work? Does it bother you?

I don't think so. That is my life. Not so happy sometime, but what can I do?

You can be a maid again.

(*A look of shock and disgust crosses her face*) No. I will not be a maid again. I cannot do that. This is better than maid. People treat maid like dirt.

What about the sex, does that make you feel bad?

No. Not bad, not good. I have sex with man for short time, it is what I must do. I don't feel good, I don't feel bad.

And the future? How long can you do this?

Until I am not beautiful anymore (*laughing*). Then I must go home. I don't know. I send some money to my family every month. They put in the bank. But I don't want to go home. My mother take care my sons. I like to live in Bangkok. So maybe I will try to find some job here in restaurant. I can cook Isaan food. Make *somtam* very delicious. Then I think I will be happy in my life.

Okay. What about this book I am writing – do you think it's a good idea? Anything you want to say to people who will read it?

Good idea? I don't know. Who will read it, someone who want to come to Thailand? Up to them to come here. Yes, I want to say come to Thailand, I will be here and wait for my bus. Every night.

6

KWAN: "IF I WAS RICH OR HAD GOOD LUCK I WOULD NOT HAVE THIS LIFE"

I met Kwan at a coffee shop down the street from where she works as a waitress 29 nights a month – in a beer bar outside a popular nightclub. If she meets a customer who likes her and wants to pay the bar fine (600 baht), she can go with him for the night. She looks tired when we meet at 3pm, but says she's fine. As the interview goes on I get the sense the tired look is not from a lack of sleep, but from life.

Q: Hi Kwan, thanks for coming to meet me. Can you tell me about yourself – where you are from, how old you are, how did you start working at the bar?

Kwan: I come from Samut Prakan, very near to Bangkok. I am 29 years old. I have been working at this bar for about four years. I came here to work because I cannot find a better way to pay for my daughter to go to school and grow up.

How old is your daughter, and where is she?

She lives with my mother in Samut Prakan. She is 12 years old and goes to school. I see her one time every two, three month. She is very smart and good student. I hope she never have to work in a bar like me.

So you don't like working in the bar?

For me, I don't mind. I have to pay for my daughter, so it is what I do. My mother must stay home to care about her at the house. My mother not have a husband, he die about three year ago from cancer.

Was that your father?

No, my father die when I am young. He was work on construction and have accident, get hurt and cannot do anything; cannot move. And die soon, maybe one week after accident.

I'm sorry to hear that. It must have been hard for you and your mother. Do you have any brothers or sisters?

I have one sister, older than me [by] two year. She go to school and finish and get married and have three children, but live far away. You know Pai? It is in the north. Her husband come from there. She live on a farm there with him.

Is it okay to ask you where your daughter's father is?

Her father die when she is young. He walk home drunk one night because lose motorcycle and truck not see him, run him over. Die. I got married again about three year after that, but my second husband, I find out he married already, so I leave him and live with my mother.

Your second husband was already married when you married him?

Yes, he have another wife in another city. I don't know about that for about six month. Then one night he drunk and tell some friend and they tell me. It's okay, he [was] not good man after we married. Drink too much, not work. I have to work in factory, then take care [of] house. So he go and I stay with mother. But cannot take care [of] daughter and mother so I come to Bangkok and work.

And was this your first job in Bangkok?

No, first I work big Thai restaurant, but no money. I try to work in disco over there – but no job, so I come here and they tell me sure, can work waitress, and can go with customer for more money.

What did you think about that?

I think, oh I know about this kind of place. But I know I can make more money. First time I [was] afraid of *farang* customer. I cannot speak English too much. But I learn.

You said you don't want your daughter to work in a bar, but you don't mind working like this?

Yes, my daughter too smart and good to work in place like this. For me, it is my life. My husband die, and I marry wrong man, so I must work here now. But my daughter I want to have different life, I hope so.

Does anyone in your family know what you do?

NO! They only know I work waitress.

And how much more do you earn here than in the restaurant?

In restaurant it is not so bad. I can earn 7,000 baht one month. But here can earn 12,000 or 15,000 or even 20,000 if [I] have good customer.

How many men do you go with in a month?

Sometime many. If I can go every night it is good for me. More money.

And how much do they pay you?

I ask them for 1,500 short time and 2,500 long time. Sometime if they good guy and say "too much" and I need some money I say okay, pay me not so much then. Maybe 1,000 short time.

Have you ever had any bad experiences with the customer?

Bad?

Yes, was there ever a customer who didn't pay you or

treated you badly?

I don't think so. Maybe one time a guy say he cannot pay. But I call the bar and he say "okay, okay, joking".

What would have happened?

(*Laughs once*) I don't know. I think nothing I can do. But before one girl I heard story [that] she go to police and tell them man not pay. They say okay you pay us 500 baht and we go talk to him. But she not have money so cannot pay police, so they tell her will they (*they will*) get 1,500 baht from man and she get 500, they get 1,000. Police go to hotel. Go see man, come out give girl 500 baht and tell her to go back to bar. Later that man friend tell us he must give police 5,000 baht or go to jail. If true, I don't know.

How long will you do this work?

I think maybe four year. I try to save my money a little, but my daughter need so much for school and clothes and music. She learn music now. She can play *ranat ek* (*Thai xylophone*) so good. I want only for her to be good and happy.

Doesn't she miss you because you are not at home?

It is not so bad, I can see her one time every month. Some children not see mother or father long time. They work in another country or far away. But this is our life. She can understand.

Are you happy or unhappy about your life?

I am happy when I see my daughter and I think about her and how she will have different life.

This is for a book about the women of Bangkok and Pattaya who work in the bars. Is there anything you want to say about your life to the people who will read it?

(*Thinking*) No, I don't think so. I have my life, It cannot change. If I was rich or had good luck I would not have this life. But I cannot change what has happened in my life. So I will do this until I go home.

7

BEE: "WHO WOULD UNDERSTAND WHAT I FEEL WHEN I COME HOME?"

Bee works at one of the large bath massage (*ab nuat*) establishments in Bangkok, in a Thai neighborhood known for its massage and karaoke bar scene. I met up with her at a restaurant near her "shop", as she calls it. The "shop" looks much more like a Las Vegas casino. However, it has neon lights, larger-than-life posters of girls and is surrounded by Roman columns. A valet greets customers as they drive up and they are ushered along a red carpet and through large red double doors by two men in suits.

Bee is medium height and thin, with white skin. Her hair is cut just below her ears. Even though it's a hot and sunny day, she shows up wearing a long sleeved shirt and a baseball cap. "I must keep my skin white," she says. Her English is excellent, with a hint of a British accent in some phrases.

Q: Hi Bee, can you introduce yourself? How old are you, where are you from, and how did your English get to be so good?

Bee: Ha. I'm not sure about my English. But I lived in England for two years. I'm 31 years old, I come from Chonburi, it's on the way to Pattaya. But I don't come from Pattaya.

How did you come to live in England for two years, and how long ago was that?

I got a visa to visit a friend who had married an English guy. That was about six years ago. And once I was there I got a job in a bar as a waitress. Then someone told me how much money I could make as a call girl. I didn't believe it, but it was true.

So you just decided "Okay, I'll be a call girl"?

I was 25 years old. I was not a virgin. I was not stupid. In Thailand I made 8,000 baht a month working in a shopping mall. As a call girl I could make 8,000 baht a day. What would you do?

But most people would say there is a difference between working in a mall and working as a call girl.

Well, (*smiling*) then I'm not most people. For me, sex is sex. You think some woman marry a rich guy and gets a big car, nice house, money for spend on what she want – you think she not trade sex for money?

That is an old argument. The thing is you sell yourself for sex – is that okay with you?

(*Shrugs*) Yes. Okay then, okay now. You know what I have done with my life? I bought a house for my mother. My sister I pay for Thai university. Now she work in a bank – it is a good job, maybe she will work there until she is old. I do that for them. For me I start to buy a small condo. You see, I don't have a lot of gold – just one chain for Buddha and one small ring. I don't have car. But I can take (of) care my family and myself.

So you worked in England for two years, why did you come back?

I miss Thailand. And I stay over my visa, so I must come home.

And when did you start to work at ---- massage?

As soon as I get back. I know here I can make money okay. Not like England (*laughing*), but is okay.

And what is okay? Do you mind telling me how much you make in one month?

I can earn 45,000 – 50,000 baht one month.

How many men do you massage in a day?

One, sometime two.

And you have sex with all of them?

I don't fuck all of them, if you say that is sex. Some are just massage and use hand.

Who are your customers?

(*Laughing*) Men with money.

Are they Thai, Japanese, western?

Most are Thai. Businessmen. Some western guys, some Japanese, some Korean, some Chinese.

Is that why you need the white skin?

I like my skin white. My skin would be white even if I did not do this work. My grandfather is Chinese. But it is good for getting customer, yes.

So, what does your family think you do, or do they know?

No. They don't know. I told them I work in restaurant in England. Now I say I am manager [in] Thai massage shop.

And who are your friends?

I have friends. They work another job – in a disco or club.

Do you have a boyfriend?

No. I not have boyfriend for many years. It's not problem for me.

Why not?

I have my life. I enjoy. A boyfriend would be a problem for me.

Because of the job?

Yes and no. Actually I like women (*laughing*). Are you shocked? But man or woman, who would want their girlfriend to do what I do?

So are you lesbian?

I don't think I am lesbian. I don't mind man, but I like to be with a woman to make love. With a man for so many years it is just fucking. So to feel love, I will sleep with a woman.

But you don't have a girlfriend?

(*Frowning*) No, I don't.

Would you like to have one?

I don't think so, not now. I have my life, And who would understand what I feel when I come home? Another massage girl? But I do not want a massage girl for a girlfriend.

So how long will you do this? Do you think you will ever have a normal life after this?

I don't think about this. I go to work every day. I take care [of] my mother. Maybe I do this two years, three years more. Then I open a business, I don't know.

So will you ever want a usual life – to be with one person?

(*Laughing*) I don't think so. Maybe I am too old to start that now. I will be an aunt for my sister's children. She will get married next year. But when I am finish I can decide.

You have travelled. You are intelligent. What do you think about the sex business in general?

(*Thinking*) I know there are bars, go-go bar. The massage is to take care of a man, relax. More than sex. **But why is the sex business so big here?**

It is big in England, too. I know. I could fuck three, four guys a day there if I want. So it is not [just] Thailand, sex is everywhere. But is big in Thailand because the girl need money. And many man come here because the weather is good, and the girl is cheap.

Is it a bad thing for Thailand?

(*Thinking*) I don't know. Many thing good and bad for country. Drugs are bad for everyone. People who rob are bad for country. Some people in England don't want Asian and Indian people to be there. They were very mean to us sometimes. So is sex bad? I don't think so.

And what do you think about this book that I am working on – asking women in the business about their lives? Is it a good idea, a bad idea?

Yes, it's a good idea. I'm not a 500 baht bar girl, I don't know what they are like. Maybe they are on drugs, or need money. Many prostitutes in England were on drugs. Cocaine, heroin, ecstasy. Where I work it is not like that. We are not drunk girls, do not have disease. Yes, this is a good idea, to talk about this life. I would read this book (*laughing*).

8

Maem: "The drug have me forget what I do, what I am"

Yaba. It's a form of amphetamine popular with some, although, surprisingly, popular with only a few of the women involved in prostitution. It is relatively cheap, gives a quick buzz and allows the user to leave their world for a brief time. Maem is "25 or 26", but looks ten years older. She's short and frighteningly skinny. Her nails are bitten to the quick and unpolished. She chain smokes and has a nervous habit of constantly looking over her shoulder (I interviewed her at a friend's apartment). I offered to buy her food, but she declined, drinking a beer over ice. She was the only woman I interviewed who insisted on being paid before she started talking with me.

Q: Hi Maem, thanks for coming to talk with me. Can you tell me about yourself? How old are you, how long have you been working?

Maem: Maem is my name. I am 25 or 26 years old.

I have been working this time for two years. Before I had a boyfriend for about one year, but I work before that for three years, I think. Yes, I start when I am about 19.

Where do you come from?

I come from Nong Kai, in north Thailand, near Laos. My family is good; my father have a shop there that sells things for tourist – things people in town make, stamps, coins. He learn English when a war was in Vietnam and Laos. I learn to speak English from him and the customers. I also learn in school.

Why did you come to Bangkok?

When I was 17 I want to leave Nong Kai and come Bangkok. I want to have something for my life, and I am boring (*bored*) in Nong Kai. So I take the train to Bangkok and come to hairdressing school here. Then I get a job right away. But it was hard. I worked six, sometimes seven days a week – cut and wash hair. I do not make much money.

Then I meet another girl come from Nong Kai who tell me about go to disco to meet foreign men. She said they pay 1,000 baht or more to sleep with me. Before I had a Thai boyfriend and I'm thinking a man crazy to pay that much to sleep with a woman. I hear before there are places in Nong Kai, but there Thai and Lao (*Laotian*) men pay 100 or 150 baht for a short time in a room with a girl.

So I start to go to disco with my friend. She introduce me to people she knows, and I speak English okay, it easy for me. To meet the men. To sleeping with them was not too hard. I only go with the men I want to. And never go for lower [than] 1,500 baht a night. If man look rich I ask for 2,500, maybe I get 2,000. I can make more in one night sleeping with man than I can one week to cut hair. I quit job and only go out with men.

Sometimes I meet a man and he take me to Phuket or Jomtien for weekend, sometimes more. I put money in bank, and save a lot - I have more than 150,000 baht save. True. Then I meet a man while I was with another man in Phuket. This guy was American man and he ask me if I know where to buy ecstasy – the drug, you know? I go out with him to buy at disco. I leave the man I stay in Phuket with, and go with this guy for the week. It was terrible mistake. I stay with him for about one year. When that time finish I am taking ecstasy and yaba every night. All the money I save is gone.

(*At this point Maem starts to get upset. She takes a long drink of water and takes a quick walk around the apartment to calm down.*)

Okay Maem, can you tell me what happened after that?

He go home to America and I try to go back to disco I go before, but I look ugly and people know I am not the same. I find small room to stay in. I have to start work, so I go to different bars, not nice like the disco, but I go in the afternoon and get a customer, come back in the bar six o'clock, find another man, and go back [at] ten o'clock, try another man. If they don't want to pay 1,000 baht I say, "Okay, 700". Now, if I want yaba, I go for 500 baht, but only for smoking (*slang for oral sex*).

Maem, do you want to get out of this life?

One and a half years ago I go to jail – three months. I am with Thai man on a motorcycle in Klong Toei (*a slum area known for drug trafficking*) and we have accident. He try to run, and some people stop him. Police come. He have a lot of drugs in his jacket. I don't even know him, but they don't believe me. They say they see me with him before and know I am addict. I try to tell police my parents are dead. I don't want them to know. Did they know ever? Yes, but I tell them [it was] only a mistake. I stay in jail for three months, then came out. I try not to do drugs now. I know it not good for me, but I'm bored, so what else can I do?

After I finish with a man, yaba have me forget what I do, what I am. Sure I want another life, a different life. But now, I cannot.

What do you think will happen in the future? Do you ever think about what you will do in five, ten years time?

In ten years what will I do? I don't know. I hope I am still not working, but I cannot see something else now for my life. I don't like it, but sometimes I think about what has happen with me. My family is good family. I not go back [to] Nong Kai for two years. I miss my family, yes. I talk with Mama and Papa on the telephone. I tell them I am good, okay. Have a job I cannot leave. I know they are very sad sometimes that they cannot see me. But if they do, I think they will feel sad more. I wish I can go back to Nong Kai and start again. But now this is my life, so what can I do?

So you want help for your problem with drugs, Maem; to go to a hospital?

No. I am okay now. But now I have to go to work. I am sorry.

UPDATE: Later I learned from two of the girls, who I had seen Maem with on previous occasions, that she had been arrested for selling ten yaba pills to an undercover policeman. She had been sentenced to one year in prison, and had been there about six months when I got the news.

9

FAH: "I GIVE SEX, HE GIVE MONEY"

Fah has curly brown hair that is cut just above her shoulders. She meets me in a new shopping mall in the city of Pattaya. She has a round face, and a beaming smile. She's wearing a low cut t-shirt, tight jeans and spike heels. She has either an expensive watch or a good copy of an expensive watch on her left wrist, and a gold bracelet on her right. She has tanned skin; in fact looks like she's just come in from the sun, something Thai women usually avoid. I notice she has old razor scars running horizontally across her left arm, from inside her elbow down to her wrist. I had been introduced to Fah the evening before at the beer bar where she works. She said she would be happy to talk with me, but had a customer picking her up, so we agreed to meet the following afternoon. Her English was relatively fluent so we did not need a translator for most of the interview.

Q: Hi Fah, thank you for coming to see me.

Fah: Yes, nice to meet you again.

Well, I told you yesterday I would like to know about your life, so can you begin by telling me where you are from, how old you are, how long you have been working in the bar?

Yes, I am 36 year old (*laughing*); do I look more than 30? I hope not! I come from Yasothon, it is in northeast Thailand. Where I come from it is poor. I lived in a small village outside the town, maybe 100 people live there. I live in the same small house for many year, until I am 17. I have stayed in Pattaya now for about one and a half year. That is this time. I lived here before for three year also. Now I have been working at the ---- Bar for about one and a half year.

Is Pattaya where you started working in bars?

First I work in massage. That was before. I have a job in Thai massage in Khan Kaen (*one of the largest cities in the northeast*), but I learn I can make more money in Pattaya and get a job doing *ab nuat* shower massage.

So you are a masseuse?

Yes, I learn massage at school in Khan Kaen, get a job. But the money is only a little. I have two children I take care [of] by myself, so I must make more money and I go to Pattaya for more money.

You have two children? How old are they and where are they?

73

My son is 16 year old, he live with me in Pattaya. I have daughter 18 year old, she stay in Chontaburi (*large city in eastern Thailand*) with husband. She been married two year already.

Okay, I have to ask – does she have any children yet?

Yes, she have a son about one year old.

So you are a grandmother?

(*Laughing*) Yes, oh my God that is true. But I am not old, not yet.

So what did you do before – you said you lived in your house until you were 17. You grew up there. And you left when you had your daughter?

I live with parents and older brother, he now about 50 year old. We are very poor. Have a small house. Two room. The toilet is outside. And shower outside. No have a kitchen, only, what you say, barbeque? I cannot go to school. No money for uniform or shoe or book. I feel sad because other children go to school and play, I stay home and help Ma with many small job – dry the pepper, sew some shirt, clean some pot for restaurant near house.

Wait, you never went to school?

Have lady live near to our house, she help me to read, write, even maths. She give me book, she is very nice. One time she give me bicycle. I am so happy then.

But I have friends, we play, work. When I am 16 year old I have a boyfriend, and I got married when I am 17 year old. I have my daughter when I am 18 year old. My husband was 20 year old, we got a job for making plastic – for window – in factory near Bangkok. We stay in small room, but have good life. Many people from Isaan work in the factory and live with us. Work is hard but everyone enjoy. I have my daughter after about one year. Then I stop work at the factory, open small shop to sell fruit outside factory. I have my son about two years after I have daughter.

Then my husband meet a new lady, and he leave me. I have two children and husband leave. I am 21 year old. I get married and have children because that man want to marry and have children. Then he leave me for woman also about 18 year old. I go back home to Yasothon, stay with Ma and Pa. I open small shop in my house, sell candy, water, coke, snack. I can take care [of] my children there. I stay there in my shop for many year. My children go to school. My parents get old, they die. I have my brother, he is older [than] me [by] about 15 year. He stay in Korat, never see him until parents die. Then he come and want to have house. I cannot believe. I take care Ma, Pa many year, never see him! I tell him no, this is my home, my shop. He can stay but I work very hard for shop and house. Then (*Fah is getting more animated and stops for a moment to catch her breath*) sorry, okay, one day I take children to school and come home and everything burn.

Burn? You had a fire? How?

Yes. I come home on motorcycle from the school. I see the smoke, I don't know what, and I arrive I see all the people stand around and looking, some people they try to help me with put water on fire, but lose everything in shop and house. Have no, what do you call, if have accident? Insurance, yes, insurance. Lose everything. That is when I do this (*Fah shows us the scars on her arm*).

You tried to kill yourself...

Yes, I think nothing will ever be good in my life. I work hard, I take care children, I take care Ma, Pa. For what? Someone, I know who but I cannot say, burn my shop, my house...

Your brother...?

I cannot say. I never see him again. Even now, never see him. If he die, I don't care.

So, how many years ago did this happen? And when did you cut your arms, when the fire happened or after?

Okay, this happen in about eight year ago, year 2000 maybe. My children are ten year and eight year old. I take my children to house of my friend, about five kilometre away, in another village. She is married to man from Finland. She say we can stay. But in night time I drink Thai whiskey and when go in my room there I think I cannot take care [of] my children, maybe they will find some other mother better than me. I cannot remember when I do this (*she makes a cutting motion across her left arm*) but my friend, she find me and take me to hospital.

I stay in hospital for two day; talk to doctor, see my children. They have nowhere to go, no one to take care [of them]. My friend say she can take care for only short time. But my friend she talk to husband and ask [for] money to help me. Her husband nice man and give enough for me to go to Khan Kaen and I can learn massage. So I go with children to Khan Kaen. I am very happy there. I study massage about two month and then work in massage shop. Thai massage, you know? No sex (*laughing*).

But the money is not enough. I speak with lady work massage and they tell me if [I] go to Pattaya [I] can make a lot of money, maybe 30,000 or 40,000 baht every month. I say "True?" I think they lie to me. In Khan Kaen I make about 8,000 baht. They tell me [it] is true, I can go [to] Pattaya and massage for *farang* or Chinese man and the salary and tip is very good (*laughing*). But must do sex with customer. I ask what they think about that. They think is not so bad. Have one lady she call another friend in Pattaya, I send photo and the shop in Pattaya tell me "come on". So I go [to] Pattaya and work ab nuat. My children stay with me in room near shop. They like Pattaya: see the beach and everything *tunten* (*exciting*) for them. I work massage there almost three year. My life good. My children go to school, my salary and tip good! One day I am drive motorcycle near the beach and BOOM, one truck hit me. I fall down, hurt very bad. What you say, sleep? Knockout, yes knockout. One day. You see here? (*At this point Fah shows me her front teeth, which I hadn't noticed before, which are chipped*) And here (*Fah pulls her hair back to show a scar where it looks as though someone has tried to cut her lower ear off*) and here (*turns over her right elbow to reveal a deep scar covering her entire elbow*), and my leg here to here (*points to just below her hip and to the side of her shin*) have a lot of blood. I stay in hospital about one week. Have some customer from massage take care [of] me, pay bill. I cry, how can they do that for me? More than 30,000 baht they pay for me. When I leave hospital I cannot work massage again. I cannot move leg the same, so cannot massage. (*In Thai Fah explains that because her leg muscles were damaged in the accident, she cannot stay in one position long enough to massage any more*). I worry, have children to take care [of], what can I do? Another customer he tell me can talk to owner at ---- Bar and can get me job. I go to Chontaburi to rest, stay with my daughter and her husband. Yes, she meet nice man, family has business there about selling fruit. So now I have been come back to Pattaya working one and a half year.

In the bar?

Yes. My son he want to stay [in] Pattaya. He have a good school here. I work the bar.

And how do you feel about the job?

(*Gives a questioning look*) How do I feel? It is my job. Sometime is good, sometime is not so good.

What is your average day like?

I come to work [at] 11:30. Get dressed for bar, sit and wait for customer. Customer come in maybe 12 o'clock. Talk with customer. Ask to buy drink for me. Yes, if buy drink I get 50 baht. And if I like customer I can ask to pay bar and take me to room upstair for sex. How much? For short time upstair, pay bar 300 baht and pay me, up to customer, but more than 500 baht. If want to take me away bar for long time, pay bar 500 baht, pay me more than 1,000 baht.

Okay, you are a mother and a grandmother – how do

you feel about selling sex?

(*Another quizzical look*) No. It is my job. I take care [of] the customer.

Do you think there is anything wrong with selling sex? What do you think about your customers?

My job is my job. Why something wrong with that? I know many people think bad about lady work bar, but look how many lady work bar in Pattaya. Man want to have sex, I give sex, he give money, I take care [of my] son. Some person get *dat pom* (*haircut*). Pay for cut hair, they take care [of] family with money. Same [for] me.

But many people would say sex is different than a haircut...

For the customer yes; for me, no.

Does that mean you don't like having sex?

(*Fah shrugs her shoulders, then thinks a moment*) Sometimes I like [it]. (*Shrugs her shoulders again*) Sometimes I like the customer, I like sex. Many time not enough time to like. Just make customer finish and get money and find new customer. But if customer nice, funny, give a good tip, then yes, like everything.

But you don't know about the tip until the end, right?

Sometime [I] ask how much they pay. Sometime customer tell how much they pay.

So what do you think about the customers? What do you think about them paying for sex? Have you ever had a boyfriend who was a customer?

The customer are a customer. Not a boyfriend. I have customer get angry [with] me for go with another man. What can I do? You pay for me every month 40,000 baht, I will stop working bar.

You make 40,000 baht a month?

Sure. Yesterday I have two customer. (*Fah looks in her purse and pulls out a small notebook, flips a few pages and studies it*) Four lady drink, 200 baht for me. Short time bar fine, 150 baht for bar and customer give me 600 baht. [long time] 250 baht for bar, customer pay [me] 1,200 baht. 2,400 baht for one day. (*She pushes the notebook with figures in it across the table.*)

That's pretty good math for someone who never went to school.

Thank you (*big smile*). And customer give me 100 baht for telephone card and 100 baht for petrol for motorcycle and buy food and drink.

But no boyfriend?

No, I will take care [of] myself and my son, then my son and daughter can take care [of] me. I don't need boyfriend. Maybe I will be lonely a little, but I think it is better stay with my son only now. Maybe when I stop work in the bar, okay, I will look for a boyfriend or husband.

When will you stop working in the bar. Soon?

I don't know. When no customer want me anymore (*laughing*). I think I can work at the bar about three more year, then my children take care [of] me. Maybe I have my own bar – "Fah Bar" (*laughing*).

Do your kids understand what you do? Do you think it bothers them?

They know I work in bar. I don't tell them I go for sex, they don't ask me.

What if they did ask you? What if your daughter lost her job, would it be okay with you if she worked in a bar?

Yes, she can work in bar if she want. It not make her bad person. You have good lady who work in bar, you have bad lady work somewhere like restaurant or hotel. Why work in bar make you bad person? We have good heart. If she have to work bar, it her life, what she must do. I not think bad about her.

What do you think of a book that tells the stories of women who work in bars and massage here in Thailand?

Sure, good idea. Many people think we are bad. We are not bad. You think I am bad? If I can be a movie star or singer I will be a movie star or singer. If I can be a rich person, I will be a rich person. But I am a poor girl from Isaan. Sometime my life good, sometime hard. But my life will be okay, I am strong (*smiling and nodding*).

UPDATE: Fah called me to say she was no longer working at the bar. She says she has invested in a noodle stand and is now selling noodles on the street outside a market in Pattaya.

I ask her if she is done at the bar and she says:

Now I am done at bar. I will sell noodle with my friend and have a different life.

So you are done with the sex business?

(*There is a pause on the phone*) I am not working there now. I want to try this with my friend. I hope I will not work at bar again. But we cannot make so much money doing this, so sometime a customer call me and want me to go with him after I finish noodles, I go. Why? Money. Money, money, money.

10

JEN: "LIKE A MOVIES"

Jen is a nude dancer in a go-go bar in one of the big entertainment plazas. She is tall and thin with dark skin and long black hair. Her eyes are small and wary. She is wearing a cut-off t-shirt which displays a large dragon tattoo on her lower back, and a pair of shorts that reveal two large scars on her left knee – they look like the marks of an injury that you would expect to see on the knee of a veteran football player. Jen's are the result of a motorcycle accident. She has a habit of narrowing her eyes when thinking about her answers, as if she is trying to sense if the person she is talking to believes her. Almost every answer was followed with *kow-chai-mai*? – do you understand?

Q: Jen, please tell me about yourself – how old are you, how long have you been working as a dancer?

Jen: I am 19 year old. I have been dancer in Bangkok about two year. First time in bar Patpong (*the infamous entertainment area, now filled mostly with booths that sell counterfeit goods),* now I work here maybe six month. Here is better. Patpong make more money, but too many problem with bar, with customer. Problem like bar charge too much for lady drink. And customer there get drunk too much. Here is better.

You just said that you are only 19, but you have been working for two years. Don't you have to be 20 to work in a bar?

My sister older is more than 22. I have her ID card, so no problem.

Where do you come from?

I come from a place in Isaan, name Si Saket. It is poor. My family does not have money, but they very good people. I have my papa and mama and two sisters and two brothers. I miss them. Too much sometimes. I go to visit family maybe three, four time last year, I think. But I do not want them come to see me. I tell them I working in market (*laughing*). I think my mama know about what I do, but she not say anything to me.

What do you think about your work? Do you like dancing?

I like this job. I like dancing. Not the same like I first start dance. I am very shy before. I have to think I am not dancing without my clothes, and so the men look at me dancing I feel shy. Now, it is really no problem for me. I like the music. I like to meet nice *farang*, have them buy me drink and take me out.

How about the other girls here – are you friends with them?

I like the other girl here. Almost all girl is very nice. Sometimes a girl maybe drink too much, then the boss tell her "Okay, one time, okay, but cannot drink too much again at work." I think one time or two time girl take drugs, but the boss tell them cannot work here, so they go.

What do you do for fun?

I don't know. Sometime go to disco, or only go home, watch TV. Go shopping. Clothes, jewellery. Go to movie. Good Thai movie, or maybe *farang* movie like some romantic story. *Titanic*, you know? All Thai girl love *Titanic*. Love story, romantic movie, very good.

How long did you go to school?

When I live in Si Saket I go to school, I stop when I am 14 year old. Now I cannot go to school. Yes, I would like to go school and learn English. Everyone say if learn speaking English can get a good job, and I not have to be dancing. But to go school cost money, and I need money to live, so I have to work.

Your bar has sex shows – do you ever work in those?

Yes, our bar has shower show – lesbian show. I try one night when one girl not come to work. I got paid 100 baht, but I don't like it. So I not do it again.

How much money do you earn at the bar?

I get salary 8,000 baht (*per month*), but if girl is late, or not come to work, not sell drinks, the bar take some salary. Man pay the bar fine, pay me, I make good money, okay? Maybe in one month I can make 20,000 baht. Sometimes more.

How many men do you go with in one month?

Different, sometimes maybe two in one week, sometimes more. Sometimes stay with man for more than one night. Last year one man take me to Phuket [for] Christmas. Very good man. I tell him I want 10,000 baht for one week. He say "no problem". We go to island, ride boat. He live Switzerland. He write me before. He tell me he come back for me and next time we go someplace nice, and maybe he take me back Switzerland one month. I hope he not lie. But if he not come, he not come.

Do you worry about AIDS or other diseases?

Yes, I am afraid [of] AIDS. I think every girl scare about it. No, not talk too much about it. I tell every man use condom. Switzerland man? No, after two times, not use. Because I trust him. And Switzerland good country. Not same Germany and England, America.

I hope that foreign men who read this book learn more about what Thai women working in bars think about their lives. What would you want to say to foreign men?

Be nice to the girl. We like to have good time. But do not tell me "I love you" if you not love me. We know you lie. "I like you" okay. Not love.

What do you think you want for your life in ten years time?

In ten year what do I want? Not sure. A good life, go away from here – the bar. Some girl go to other country, but they come back. I think it is not so easy to live away from Thailand. Some girl go to America, Canada, Europe. I only want nice life in Thailand. Maybe meet nice man who want to stay here. Live near beach someplace. And, yes, not work in bar. I think it nice to love one man forever. Like a movies.

11

Newie: "Some day it will be better"

Newie works in a massage parlour that caters to Korean, Japanese and Western customers. She is short and stocky, with very light skin. She wears no make-up. Her eyes are large and round, her nose is thin. She smiles a lot during the interview and her smile is one that lights up the room.

Q: Hello Newie, thank you for talking with me. Can you tell me about yourself – how old you are, where you come from?

Newie: I am 23 years old. I come from NongKai, near Laos.

How long have you been working here?

Here, I have been working for less than one year. Before I work massage about one year.

And here you give Thai massages, but is there also sex?

Yes. If customer want to have special massage we can give.

Does it bother you or make you feel bad, to have sex with customers?

Sometime, yes. Depend on customer. If they are good customer, it is okay. When I start to do this business, I always feel bad, but now, maybe bad not much.

What do you think about the customers?

I don't think about them. This is my job. They come here for massage and service. My job is for their service.

How did you get started in massage – did you have a job before, or did you go to school?

No, I stop to go to school when I am 11 year old. My family have no money, so I must stop. I help my family with selling things at market, then when I am 15 I go to work as *coolie*.

What do you mean by *coolie*?

I work construction. Make a house. You see – I am strong *(laughing, she grabs my arm and squeezes – she is surprisingly strong)*. I can do construction no problem. But then they have no more work, so I come to Bangkok to look for job. Have a job, but not pay money enough. So I go to work massage.

How much money did you make working in construction, and how much do you make here?

Construction in Bangkok I make about 4,500 baht every month. And work very hard. Everyday. Go to work maybe seven in the morning, finish [at] six or seven. Can do nothing but come back to the place where we stay, eat and go to sleep.

So this is better?

(Laughing) YES! More money! And not so tired everyday.

How much more money do you earn?

I earn here about 10,000 baht per month.

And where do you live?

I live here. Upstair. Have some room for the girl who work here (*there are rooms upstairs for the girls who work here*).

You have your own room?

No. I never have own room in my life. I stay with three other girl.

In one room?

Sure. We can stay together. We don't have problem.

And what about the other massage parlour? Why did you leave there?

My friend tell me this is better. Other massage okay, but money is not so good. Sometime make only 4,000 or 5,000 baht one month.

What about your family? Do they know what you do?

My family think I do Thai *(legitimate)* massage. They don't know I do this. I send them money every month to take care [of them].

Do you have any children?

No, not yet. I am never married. So I don't have any children,

What about the future? How long do you think you will work here? Do you want to get married and have a family?

Of course I want to get married. I would like to meet a nice man and have a family so someone can take care [of] me. I always take care [of] everyone since I was little. I hope someday someone can take care [of] me, too. Maybe I will work here one or two years, then I hope I have enough money to go home. Have a business in my hometown. Now I can speak English, so it's good for a business in Nong Khai. We have a lot of foreigner come there. So I think if I have a business like tour or guest house I can have a good life.

Would you like to marry a Thai or a foreigner?

As long as good man and can take [care of] me, I don't care; can be Thai, Chinese, Japanese, English. But have to take care [of] me and be good man. And take care my family, too.

Is there anything you want to say to people who read this book about your life?

What about my life? I don't think anyone want to know about my life. I am just one person, cannot read, cannot write, can only do massage and *coolie*.

**Well, what do you think of your life? Are you happy?
Should people feel sorry for you?**

I don't want anyone have to feel sorry for me. I'm
strong. Strong hands, strong heart (*laughing*). My life
is okay. Someday it will be better life I think. I believe
that.

12

Lin and Dah: "Someday [we] will leave this life and have a good life"

Lin and Dah are sisters. They work out of two "beer-bars" on one of Bangkok's main tourist strips. They arrive for work anywhere from 10:00pm to 1:00am, and stay until one or both find customers – some nights that can be five in the morning. Dah is 22, a bit overweight, with a round, plump face and wide oval-shaped eyes. She wears a lot of make-up, which makes her appear older. Lin is 19, thin, but with the same round face and eyes. She has her hair cut just below her ears, and wears little make-up. Dah speaks excellent English and Lin speaks it fairly well, although she is shy and lets Dah do most of the talking, unless she is asked a question directly. They are both cheerful, and look at each other and laugh throughout the interview. I spoke with them at a restaurant before they set off to their regular spots at the bar.

Q: Hi Dah, hi Lin, can you tell me where you come from?

Dah: We are from Bangkok, we live near the old airport, with our parents and brother and Lin's baby.

Were you born in Bangkok?

Dah: Lin was born in Saraburi. I was born in Bangkok. We have lived in our house since Lin was a baby. (*Lin pokes her younger sister in the ribs and laughs*)

Is your brother older or younger, and what does he do?

Dah: He is 16. He goes to school – a good boy.

Do your parents or brother know where you go every night?

Dah: They do not ask now. Before I tell my mother we work in restaurant. I think maybe they know, but not want to talk. No, never ask where money come from. We only leave in box for my mother.

Lin, can you tell us about your baby – do you have a boy or a girl and how old are they?

Lin: I have baby girl, daughter. She is now four years old. She is very smart, she will go to school next year I think. Yes, the father is Thai man, my boyfriend before, but now I never see him. He leave me about maybe two years ago. I think he have a wife, but not sure. So I must take care of my baby.

95

How many nights do you both work? And Lin, who takes care of your daughter when you come to work?

Lin: My mother take care. It is no problem for her.

Dah: Sometimes we come to work every night, but if we have enough money, we not come to work. How much is enough money? Not sure *(looks at her sister, they both smile and shrug)*, enough to give to my parents and brother. To help with food, rent, and their shop.

How much do you make in one month?

Dah: Not sure – sometimes not the same all the time. Lin have more customer than me *(they both laugh)*.

Okay, Lin how much do you make in one month?

Lin: I can say if many *farang* come to bar, about 25,000 baht in one month.

Is that together or just you?

Lin: Only me. Dah make how much? *(laughing)*

Dah: Maybe not that much. *Farang* like Lin, she skinny, I am fat *(laughing)*.

Lin: Not true, only a little fat. But have *nom yai (big breasts)* – *farang* like too much! *(she gives one of Dah's breasts a squeeze – they both start laughing)*

Do you always have this much fun together?

(Dah and Lin look at each other and make faces)

Dah: Yes, we are like this together all the time.

Lin: Sometimes serious.

Serious about what?

Lin: Want to change our life sometime. In this life there are good and bad people. I think we are good people.

Who are good people – you and Dah, or all the girls?

Lin: I know for Dah and me, good people. Do not smoke, or drink too much, or steal. And we want to stop work like this someday.

Dah: Yes, I want to finish my school and get a good job.

Dah, you go to school now?

Dah: Yes, I go to school to learn about secretary. I go more than one year already.

Lin, do you go to school?

No, I stop school after I am pregnant – I am 16 years old then.

Did you learn to speak English in school? Both of you speak very good English.

Dah: I learn some in school, but learn most from talking to foreign man.

Lin: Same.

How did you start working, and why did you start?

Dah: We have a friend tell us we can make money if we meet *farang* in a bar. She is working for about one year, have some nice things.

Dah: Yes, we have no money from working with mother and father, and so we want money to have life like some friends.

What kind of life is that?

Dah: I want to have fun, and pay to finish my school. Get a job like secretary or reception.

Lin: I like to go to beach, mountains with friends. And go to shopping.

And you cannot have that life some other way?

Dah: (*Thinking*) Maybe in the future, not now.

Lin: No. When work like this we can give money to parents and have money for us, not have to ask parents for money.

What did you think when your friend told you about what you have to do to make the money?

Dah: Good idea for money, bad idea for work.

Lin: I need money for my baby, and we want to help family.

Why do you think it's a bad idea for work?

Dah: Not good for lady to work like this. Sometimes not a good job, but for money, okay.

Lin: Don't like to go with man who can give a problem to lady – get angry or not pay.

Dah: Before many times scared of *farang*. Now we do not go if not a nice man.

Is there anything you like about doing this besides the money?

Dah: Sure, many times meet nice man, go to movie, go to eat, go to disco for dancing. Meet many different *farang*, speak English with them. Many are good man, tell a joke, have a good time.

Lin: Maybe can meet a good man for husband (*both start giggling*). I hope I can do that.

What do you think about the customers – do you remember them, do you like them?

Dah: Yes, I remember them. Many are good, but I don't like any that talk bad to the women, or drink too much.

Lin: Yes, I remember them too. And I think the same – if drink too much or say and do bad things, then no good. I think many are good person.

What about having sex – do you ever like it, or is it only for money?

Lin: I do not. I like to be with a man if he is nice, but not for make love.

Dah: Me, okay, I can enjoy to make love with nice man. If he is nice, and I know he will pay a lot of money! (*Both start laughing again*)

Do either of you have or want a boyfriend – either Thai or foreign?

Dah: No. But I am thinking about it. I think I would like one – *farang* or Japanese. Thai man no good. Drink, never come home.

Lin: No boyfriend. I don't want boyfriend. I want husband. Yes, I think the same about Thai man.

Okay, you said you had no money working for your mother and father. What work did you do for them?

Dah: Work for the shop they have near our home – sell flowers.

So is it better to work here? Was it bad working for them?

Dah: Boring. Nothing to do. Wait in shop and watch TV. Clean shop.

Isn't working like this boring – to do the same thing every night?

Dah: Yes, some times if there are no *farang* to talk to, it is boring. But if we talk to men, it is not.

Lin: Sometimes boring, but if I do not like, I can go home, not have to work. Up to me.

How much does a man pay to go with you?

Dah: Can be not the same all the time. I say I want them to pay 1,500 baht for short time. I cannot go all night because our mother worry if we not come home.

Lin: Same. Sometimes if no customer I will say okay for 1,000 baht for short time, but cannot go with man if he does not pay so much. More? Yes!!! (*laughing*)

What is the most money a man has given you?

Lin: 4,000 baht. Good man (*laughing*). And one man take me to Phuket, for one week give me 10,000 baht.

Dah: And we have two men take us to Pattaya for three days, give about 7,000 baht for each. Pay for hotel, food, movie, disco.

So you want to stop working sometime – do you think about how long you will work like this?

Dah: Maybe one year, maybe two years.

Lin: The same.

Dah: If you work like this you meet good and bad people. I am afraid it is hard to stop this life if work too long. I hope when I finish this work I can stop thinking about what I do here.

Do you have a dream or a plan for your future?

Dah: Finish school and get a good job.

Lin: Take care [of] my family and [my] baby. Maybe have a shop one day – but not flowers (*laughing*). I think a restaurant would be good.

Dah: I would like to have money in my bank and be with family.

What do you think about the idea for this book – to let the girls talk about their working lives – and what do you think the book should say?

Dah: I think maybe it is a good idea. But many girls do not want to talk about this life. The job is not a good one. Can Thai people read this book? Thai people do not look at this life in a good way. Maybe you can write about problem for girl in Thailand – no work, no good opportunity for the future.

Lin: The book can say I am looking for good husband *(laughing)*.

Sure, no problem. Is there anything else you want to say to the people who will read this – maybe it will be customers.

Dah: Be a good and kind man when you are with me. Then I can like you and enjoy.

Lin: Do not think that because we do this we are not good persons. We can have a kind heart and good heart if you are the same.

Dah: A life with family is not the same as this – it is different life. If you work like this you have to know this is a different life, and someday you will leave this life and have a good life.

UPDATE: I ran into Dah about a year after this interview. Dah had finished school, but had not yet looked for a job – she claimed Lin did not want to work alone. I asked her when she thought she would stop working and for the first time since I began talking to her a year before, her face fell. "I don't know," she said, "I have to go now, Lin is wait me at the bar."

13

NAT: "BETTER THAN THE FACTORY"

Nat is 27 years old and works at a beer bar in a tourist area. She is short and very nondescript. Her black hair comes to her shoulders, she's slightly built and wears no make-up. She's wearing a loose fitting t-shirt, cargo pants and flip-flops. Nat has a wary look upon her face, as if she doesn't believe that someone is paying her to simply sit and talk. My translator notices the same look and tries to reassure her...

Q: Nat, can you sit and talk for awhile? I just want to ask you a few questions about your work and your life? Is that okay?

Nat: Yes, I think so.

Good, can you tell me about yourself? How old are you, where do you come from?

I am 27 year old. I come from Bang Phlii, not so far from Bangkok.

When did you come to Bangkok, and why?

I come to Bangkok about two year ago.

Why did you leave Bang Phlii?

Nothing to do there, work in factory for small money, get old, have Thai man not work, lazy, drink, gamble. Here is better – work in beer bar. Play pool, drink, talk with customer, not serious.

So in Bang Phlii you had a job and boyfriend or husband?

Yes, I work in factory there. Have Thai boyfriend. Same I say, same friend – he no have job; drink, play card, snooker all night. Take my money. So I leave him, come here to work bar.

How did you know about working in a bar?

I have friend in Bang Phlii, she work bar over there (*pointing*). She not complain, talk about some good man, some bad man, but money is good.

So how does the money compare to money earned working in a factory? Was she telling the truth?

Yes, she not lie. Factory salary about 6,000 baht in one month. In bar I can make same salary but get tip and if go with man 1,500 baht (*per month*) or more.

And how long have you been in the bar, two years?

Yes, since I come from my home.

And what is the most money you have made in a month? Do you save money?

Sometime I make 25,000 baht one month. Sometime I make 15,000 baht, sometime 10,000 baht. For one year I not save money, only give to my family. Now I give money to my aunt to keep for me. Already she have about 20,000 baht.

So what do you think about working in a bar?

It is my job. Better than factory. Factory is so boring. Same every day, every time. Bar is better. Can talk with my friends, customer; sometime customer take me to some new place. It's okay for me.

Did you ever have a customer who wanted to take you away from the bar so that you wouldn't have to work here any more?

I have one man, he from England. He pay bar for me for one month and take me Phuket, Krabi for holiday. Nice man. Then he go back England, pay bar one more month. I don't go to bar, don't go with man. But after one month I tell him he must give me 15,000 baht one month so I can find job, not work in bar. He give me money one month, then tell me cannot again. So I go work in bar again.

When was this? Did you ever see him again?

About six month ago. I never see him again. I ask him on telephone why he cannot pay for me. He tell me he cannot, not enough salary. So I tell him I go back to bar. He not talk to me.

Did it make you sad?

No.

No? Anything else about him?

No. He is in England. I don't know him any more.

What if he came back and wanted to see you?

If he have money, sure.

About how many men do you go with every month?

I don't [know for] sure. Sometime in one week, maybe two times, three times.

How do you feel about going with these men, about having sex with them?

(*Thinks for a minute*) Some are very nice man. Funny. Like to enjoy something like drink, go to somewhere. To have sex I don't mind. It is what they want. They pay me to take care, so I want to make them happy about that. Because good for them and good for me.

Do you mean that the sex is good for you?

The feeling of the sex? (*Shrugs*) Yes, sometime is good. If they want to make me feel good they can. But many man only want to have good feeling for them. I don't mind, that is my job. But I like to feel good, too.

Do you always have safe sex – use a condom?

Mostly times.

Do you worry about AIDS?

Sometime, but I go to clinic every month. I only have sex with no condom if I know customer.

Do you think about your future, or how much longer you will do this for?

In the future – don't know, how I can think about future now? I think about today, tonight. How I can pay my room this week.

Do you have anything you want to say to anyone who might read this book? Also, what do you think of a book about the girls who work in the bars?

I never think someone want to make a book about us. Why? We are interesting? Who will read it?

We don't know, but you can say anything about your life that you want to.

My life is my life. Sometime good, sometime hard. Sometime lonely. But I think someday I will be happy.

14

Nung: "I am the *Mamasan*"

Nung is 34 years old, but doesn't look it. She is slim, does not wear make-up, and is dressed in blue Levi's, Nike running shoes and a clean and pressed Harley Davidson t-shirt. She smiles most of the time, and has an infectious laugh. She has worked her way up the ladder in the sex trade industry – from bar girl to *mamasan* in a beer bar in one of Bangkok's western-oriented go-go bar plazas. Her English is excellent – the entire interview was conducted through English.

Q: Hello Nung – can you tell me about yourself?

Nung: I work at the Bar. I am the *mamasan*. I take care of the girls. Make sure they come to work, and are okay. If they have a problem they can come to me and I try to help them. Most of the girls have a problem with boyfriend. Sometimes have Thai boyfriend; tell them they not make enough money. Or have *farang* boyfriend want them to not work. I cannot help them with those problems. Only tell them to tell boyfriend to go away *(shakes head)*. If this is your job, then better to not have boyfriend. My bar is nice bar. Men come to sit and drink, talk with girls. If they want to take girl and girl say "Okay" then good. Bar fine is 500 baht. Girl get 200, bar get 300. If girl get ten men to take her one month, she get 1,000 baht bonus. Man pay girl whatever she want. Not business of the bar. Short-time, long-time, no problem. Up to girl and customer. Some girls, yes, go short time, come back and work again. No problem. Up to girl.

How old are you and where are you from?

Me? I am 34 years old. I am from *(named province)*, you know? I live in Bangkok now for 12 year. I have three children, live in *(named village)* Do they know my job? No *(laughing)*. I tell them I work restaurant. My older sister take care of them. Oldest boy he now 16. Big boy *(laughing)*. He come to see me last week. Grow up very fast. He is good boy. Want to join the army. Good for him. I worry sometimes, because now he can get into trouble – girls, drugs, drinking. But he is good boy. I have another boy 12 and a girl 10 year old. Girl have *farang* papa. She will be beautiful. I don't want her to work in bar. I hope she can finish school and get a good job somewhere. She wants to be policeman! Sure,

I will like that, no problem with me. Her papa? I never hear from him now. For maybe five year he send some money for her, but now nothing.

Do you have a husband?

No, my husband leave me many years before. He was not good man – like to fight, see other women. Leave my son with my mother. So we have divorce. Better that way. My son live with my mother and I live in Bangkok and send money for him.

Where do you live?

Now I live in a room near the bar. I live with two friends. We pay 4,000 baht a month for the room. No air con, but we have a fan, and a little space outside. I like it okay. Better than to live at the bar, or with five or six girls, like when I first come to Bangkok.

When was that? How did you start working in bars?

Before, first time Bangkok, I work massage. I was 17 years old. I have my son already [and] my husband tell me to get a job. I know a lot of girl come to Bangkok to work, so I come on the bus, first go to Patpong. I meet a man ask me if I can work massage. I say okay, no problem for me. But I not know about special massage (*laughing*). First time customer take my hand, put here (*points to crotch*), I say "Oh, cannot!" (*Laughing harder*). But he tell me he give me 500 baht, I say, okay. So I work massage maybe one year, then I work waitress in go-go bar, about one year. Manager ask me if I can be dancing, I say "Okay, sure". So I am dancing maybe two years. I make a lot of money. How much? It was a long time ago, and everything different then. But I have a nice apartment and send money to my home. Then *farang* ask me I want to help him in other bar, I say okay, and I am manager of bar on Soi Cowboy. But he can't pay for everything after about two and a half years, I think. So I work hostess and waitress again, and work *mamasan* now for about three or four years.

What is your salary now?

I have about 11,000 baht a month salary. Customer can buy me drink, I keep half money for lady drink. Can give me tip if I get a girl for them. But I never go with man now. (*Starts to laugh*) Oh, I lie. I have one man he take me maybe one time in two weeks. He good man, but have wife. He tell me, "Oh you are beautiful, if I not have wife I marry you". Lie. But no problem. He is good man. I have another man from Australia. He come two time every year. Stay two or three week. Pay bar for me every night. We go out. He give me money last time for my children, 10,000 baht. Very good heart. I no need to go with man. I have money.

Are you happy?

Yes, I am happy. I like to take care of the girls. I go to see my children maybe four or five times one year, they are happy. I can do what I want. I not have to work. If I want to not work for one month, two month, okay, no problem. Last year I go home for three month.

What if a man wants to take a girl out of the bar, to stop her working; can he do that?

Yes, no problem. Girl want to stop, up to her.

Does that happen a lot?

Sure, but the girl come back in one week, two weeks.

Do relationships between customers and bar girls ever work out?

Sure *(laughing)*, every night!

But for a long time?

It is not easy for the girl. We have our life – maybe many people think it is a bad life, but it is what we know. If a girl work a long time here, she never trust any man. And many girl here – a man is crazy to trust them. Men do not understand – we take care our family. I know many men *(laughing)*, from outside Thailand. They come here, see a beautiful girl, they think she will make him happy. And for a holiday sure, very happy. But he bring her to Germany or England or Australia

– she have no friends, no job. What can she do? One time I stay in Sweden for three months – the man does not want me to go to the town without him. I stay home and watch TV I cannot understand? I eat food I do not like to eat? No, Thailand is better for me. Maybe if the man will live in Thailand, speak Thai, understand Thai people. [That is] okay.

Why have a lot of girls said no when I asked them to talk to me?

Sure. Maybe they don't trust you. Maybe they not understand why you do this – talk to them about their life. Maybe they are, what is the word, guilty, that they work like this.

(While we have been talking almost every other person who passes by – women, Thai and western men, even policemen – say hello to Nung)

You have a lot of friends here...

I have many friends – girls, men; *farang* men, Japanese men, Thai men. Japanese men are nice; rich, polite – unless they are drunk, then they are stupid.

So is there a difference between Western, Japanese and Thai men?

Farang men *go-hok (lie)* but Thai men drink too much, take money, beat up wife. But girls, we are all friends. Have to take care [of] each other. If we do not, who will?

114

What do you think of a book being written about the girls' lives?

Yes, I think a book about us girls is good idea. Men come here, they want to buy a girl for a night or a week. Sometimes think we are not people. If a man respect me, I can talk with him, maybe be friends. Man talk to girls bad, no; go some other bar, go home. I respect myself now. Before, when I was young, no. But now I know about life. Why should I not respect myself? I know what I do. I do not hurt anyone. I take care of my girls, my children, my family.

What do you want for your future?

I want to save money to go back home, buy a house for me, get old and let my children take care of me *(laughing)*.

UPDATE: Just under a year after this interview I ran into Nung at another bar and stopped to see how her life was going.

Hi Nung, remember me?

Sure, yes. Nice to see you. You see I am at a new bar now.

Yes, it's nicer – and are you still the *mamasan*?

Yes, I am manager. This bar is new, have good owner, have a lot of money. More salary *(laughing)*.

But more girls and customers, too. Does that mean more problems?

Yes, before have about 10 girls, at this bar have about 20. And this bar have more customers. I am very busy in my job now *(laughing)*.

Besides the new job, has anything else happened since I last spoke with you – are your kids okay?

Yes, my son want to be in army, I tell you that, yes? And my daughter is good, too.

So, no complaints? Any new men in your life?

(Laughing) I not going to tell you – you put in the book and somebody read about me, maybe I have a problem. But I am happy *(laughing)* I got someone make me happy. And so I don't want to complain. I am very okay.

15

Joy: "We work for money, not for love"

Tonight Joy is going to go out and look for a man to sleep with. She is dressed in skin-tight black designer jeans, high heels, and a bright red, sleeveless blouse. Her shoulder-length black hair shines and her big eyes are accentuated by make-up. Her lipstick matches her blouse. She is tall, about 5'8" in her heels, and has light skin.

Q: Hi Joy, can you tell me something about you and your life?

Joy: I don't work in a bar – I did for one year, but I did not like it. I've been working going to discos and sleeping with men for three years. I am 21 year old. In the bar I was hostess – stand in front and tell men to come inside to meet some girls. What did I not like? Always have the boss tell me to get more men to come in. No it was not a go-go bar – only have a bar and girls to meet the men. Every night boss ask me "Why not so many customers?" What can I do? We are not supposed to touch them outside. But they like me and stay outside and talk with me. Sure, sometimes I go with them. Then one night I quit. I have some friends who only go to disco to meet men. So I quit and now that is what I do. My friends said that they come to disco to meet boyfriends, and it is good way to make money. They speak true about money.

Where are you from?

I come from the north – near Chiang Mai. I have been in Bangkok for four years. I went to public school but stop about 17 year old. After I go to school and learn cut hair, but there is not enough business so I go to work in the bar and now do this.

Where do you live now?

I live in room with four other girls in Bang Kapi, in Bangkok. I live in big building with many room. It very noisy, very hot. If we have open the window, too many mosquito come in. Then we cannot sleep. We pay 2,500 baht a month, 500 baht for month each girl. I wish it was big. I wish to live in a big house, and sometime I will. I try to spend only 50 baht every day for food. I do not smoke, and I only drink sometime. If a man buys me a drink, okay, but I want to save money.

Your English is excellent – where did you learn it?

You think? *Wai-ing (thank you)*. I learn in my school and then when I work in the bar I practice with customers. Now I have a book I read and study, and talk to men in disco.

Is there anything you like about this work?

The only thing I like is money. I have to save 1,500 baht every week. I have to sleep with three men in every week for this. Now it is not so hard – the tourist come, and I can sleep with man every night if I like. Some week I do. How much do they pay me? Up to them. But more than 1,500 baht for short time and more than 2,500 for all night. Yes, sometimes more *(smiling)*.

So far I have now almost 100,000 baht in the bank. In one more year I will buy a house, then open hair shop in the house. I will be the owner. No one will tell me what to do again. Who to sleep with or what time to come work. Nothing. That's what I want for my life.

What do you not like about this life?

Sometimes I have to sleep with men I don't like; I have to do things with them I don't like. I think about disease – I will not go with man who does not use condom, and I do not care how much money they say they will give, I will never change my mind. Other girl?

Some not use condom sometime. Want more money, they do not think about what can happen.

What do you think about the men – the customers?

I do not understand them, the customer. I will not go with a man and another woman. Many *farang* want that. Why I will not do that? If I want to I will, I don't want to. They want to sleep with different girls. Before I ask "You have a wife?" They say yes, and I think "Why you want to sleep with me?" But now, never mind, not bother me. I only count money. And I wonder why do they lie? Do you know how many girl think a man will come back for them? They believe different man every night.

What do you think of western men?

They are rich, they have a lot of money, but some are *kee-nee-ow (stingy)*. They want to give the girl small money if they can. They all have a big house in their country. Have I ever been there, to another country? No. But I know because the picture they show to me and from video and movie. Do I hate them? No. Do not think that. Some are okay; they want to have good time on holiday. But you understand sometime they make us feel bad, and why? We only do the best we can; for us, for our families.

What makes you happy?

When I think about when I will have my house and my shop. My young sister will work with me. She is now 17. And we will take care of our mother. My father, he die about five year ago. He got sick and die. What disease, I don't know, I think from his job. He work in a factory, make paint. He about 45 year old. The company give my mother 10,000 baht. She has a small house now, but [she is] lonely. When I go back to home she will not be so lonely. What does she think I do? I am a hairdresser *(smiling)*.

For fun, what do you and your friends do?

We go out – Thai disco and dance together. We don't want to meet Thai men. For what? They take our money and gamble, drink, go with other women. No, we have fun together. Talk a little about our life, about Thai life.

What do you think of a book about the women who work like you – is there anything you think the book should say?

I hope *farang* read this book. I want to tell them if they want to meet a Thai lady for a girlfriend or wife, better you go to a nice place and meet different kind of girl. But that other girl maybe do not want sex right now. Wait, tell the girl okay, just for the movie or eating dinner. If only want sex, okay, girl from bar is better. We work for money, not for love.

121

16

Oi: "Come with a good heart"

Oi is 24, has dark skin, a round face, with big eyes. She bounces in to meet me at 11:00am in a trendy coffee shop, which she chose as their café latte shakes are "the best". Oi could pass for an American college student: wearing a UCLA t-shirt, blue Levi's, and instead of the usual high-heeled shoes, Nike running shoes. Her hair is tied back in a short pony tail and she isn't wearing make-up.

She works in a small beer bar in one of Bangkok's large entertainment plazas. She will be heading to work at 1:00pm, where she will stay until 2:00am, unless she gets a customer to take her out earlier. That is her schedule for 28 days out of the month.

Q: Hi Oi, thank you for talking with me. Can you tell me about yourself – how old are you, where are you from?

Oi: My name is Oi. I am 24 years old. I come from Petchaboon. About five hours from Bangkok on the bus. Petchaboon very poor, where I come from. When I am 14 years old, my family can not afford my school anymore, and I not want to work in rice field, or work in garment factory sewing for my life.

So you came to Bangkok when you were 14?

Yes, 14 or 15 years old. I come with my older sister. We not know any people in Bangkok. But we get jobs with families from Hong Kong. I am a maid for about three years. The family is okay. They have three children I take care [of]. The children, they are about eight, ten and maybe 13 years old. I cook, wash clothes, shopping, and clean the house. I get 30 baht for one day, and I sleep in small room in the house. I save all the money to send home to my mother and my father. My father was work in a rice field for a boss, but he get sick and have to stop work. What was he sick with? He get malaria, and he always tired. He cannot work. My mother take care for him and my two young brothers. So my sister and me, we send our money home. My sister work for a different Chinese family, but they are no good. She leave them in about two months. She get a job in a hotel, work maid. She make about 4,000 baht in one month. She stay with some other girls from the hotel.

Me, I stay with the family three years. I work very hard, but I am happy. Better than live in Petchaboon and [be] so poor. But I miss my family too much, so I go home for one year. But no job for me. My friend Sa, who go home in Petchaboon and visit, she work in Bangkok, tell me go to Bangkok with her. She tell me I am good for *farang* men. She tell me, "you have dark skin, so the *farang* will like you." She say I can meet *farang* men, maybe find a rich husband. She tell me she sometime make 30,000 or 40,000 baht in one month. My parents make not that much in one year. Sa work in a massage parlour. Thai massage, Oil massage. You know, massage a man, give a special massage, and get good tip. She say sometimes the man can take you to hotel for night to sleep with him and I can make 1,000 or 2,000 baht for one night. I tell her I not understand, just to sleep man pay 1,000 baht? She laugh and say I have to have sex with him. I tell her I can never do *(laughs)*. I never have sex before. I have a Thai boyfriend for short time but I never have sex with him. I think we kiss one or two times. I think sex only for having children after you marry. True. And I am almost 20 years old then! But Sa talk and talk and so I come to Bangkok.

I tell her I cannot work massage, so we get job in

beer bar. I work service *(waitress)* and Sa meet customer when they come in. You know, sit with them, talk with them, and tell them to buy drinks and take her outside. She speak English good for Thai bar girl, but me, before I can say only "hello". But at the bar I learn to speak *lay-ow lay-ow (quickly)*. (*Laughing again*) "Where you come from? What is your work? How long you stay Bangkok?" At first I am very shy and cannot talk too much to the customers. But Sa help me, introduce me to customer. But I not go out with them. I think they like me because I am shy and quiet. They say they will give 2,000 or 3,000 baht for me to go with them. But I always say no. Then one time I go with nice man from England. I not tell him I am virgin; I am scared. No, not scared of man, scared because the first time, I don't know what to do. I do not know if he know I am virgin. I not tell him. He know I not know how to do. Sa and the other girls tell me a lot, and I even watch video-x (*x-rated video*) before. But doing it [is] different. In morning he give me 2,500 baht – Sa tell the price with him. I am so shy if he not give me I not ask for it. After that first time, I think, "This is easy". Now I am here for four years. I have gone with many men. Now it is no problem. If the man has good heart, okay, I have good time. I try to find out about him

125

before we go. Sure, sometime we get to hotel and man is not nice. I hope he quick, then I can go back to bar, or go home. If I am afraid of man, if I think he is bad, I tell him, "Okay, you go take shower, I wait you." Then I leave, go to bar. If he come back want bar fine return, we give him. But I think only happen maybe two times before. I never say I will stay long time (*all night*), but if he is a good man, have nice hotel, sleeping all night with him is okay.

Have you ever had a boyfriend, or wanted one of the customers to be your boyfriend?

(She thinks for a minute before answering) A boyfriend. No, never have a real boyfriend. Some man I like, but I don't know about that when I was young. Now, I know too much *(laughing)*. Have I ever fall in love? No. I like some customer before, but they are butterflies (*someone who is unfaithful*). Now I don't think I can fall in love with man who come here.

How about working with the other girls?

We *(girls)* are good together. We care about each girl. No one want another girl to have a problem. I don't drink too much, and I never take drugs. Yes, there are some girls that do, but not here at this bar. You cannot trust them. They might make a problem with the man – steal from him, or something. Then he come back to bar, and bar have a problem. No one want that. I work in small bar, only have seven girls work there, plus I think four service girls and three bartenders, everyone know everyone.

How much money do you usually make in one month?

I don't know. Sometime about 20,000 baht one month, sometime more (*smiling*). What? No, I tell the truth. I get salary 6,000 baht, and if man pay bar I get 300 (*out of 650*). Last year one man took me to Ko Samuii for one week. He pay bar for one week, and pay me 10,000 baht. It was very nice. He tell me he will come back, but I do not see him again. If he come back, okay. If not, okay, no problem.

Do your parents know what you do? Is your sister still working?

My parents? No, they do not know what I do. They know I am waitress. But nothing else. My mother always ask when I will come home and get married. I tell her, don't worry mama, I will. But now, really, I am not sure. About getting married. I want to have children, a son. But I don't want to have a son without a father. I do not trust Thai men, and the men here, *Farang* men; they come here, they cannot speak Thai, they only want sex and drink too much. Why would we like someone like that? My sister she go to Phuket with a man about one year ago, but they have fighting too much. So now she work bar in Phuket. I see her sometime if she come to Bangkok.

How do you feel about what you do? Are you tired of it?

I don't understand some of the question. I do not feel about it. Sometimes I have *mai sabaii jai* (*sad heart*), but I am good person for my family and friend.

Do you wish you could do something else?

Many people wish to do something else, right? Many girl want to be singer. Many boy want to play football. This is my job. I will finish this someday.

When is someday? What do you want in the future?

I have money in my bank. I want to stop work here soon. I will go back home to Petchaboon. Or maybe go to Phuket with my friend and sister. We want to open business for tourist. No, not bar. Maybe sell things like Thai craft.

Do you think a book about these girls of Bangkok is a good idea?

I think a book about Thai girls is good idea. *Farang* know nothing about Thai girl.

Is there anything you want to say to anyone who might read this book?

We need and want money for the family, and to have good time. Tell them that. Tell them to come here. To Thailand. With a good heart. And money *(laughing)*.

17

AAE: "MY HEART IS COLD WHEN I AM WORKING"

Aae works at one of the more infamous "sex bars" that exist in the Thailand bar scene. She lives and works in Pattaya, the beach resort town known for its nightlife. At first glance she looks younger than her 20 years, in fact I even have my translator ask to see her ID card. But as the conversation goes on it becomes clear that she is wise beyond her years. Her innocence fades. She is one of approximately 12 girls who regularly work at her bar. The girls greet customers as they walk through the door and try to entice them to go upstairs to a second bar, where the customer can get oral sex from under the bar, or a private room for sex. The price at the bar is 700 baht, of which the girl gets 350 baht; the room is 800 baht and the girls get 400 of that amount. The average tip is 100 baht at the bar, 200 baht if they go to a room. On a good day a girl will have five or six customers. If she's lucky a customer will pay the bar fine and take her out for the night. Of the 600 baht bar fine, the girl gets 250, although this goes up after a certain number of fines are paid for the girl during a given month.

Q: Hello Aae, thank you for talking with me. Can you tell me a little about yourself – how old you are, where you come from?

Aae: I come from Surin, in Isaan. I am now 20 years old.

How long have you been working in a bar?

I have worked at ---- Bar for about 10 months.

Did you work someplace else before you came to work here?

No, this is only place I work. For a bar. Before I have a job in Surin. I working in factory, sewing. I make chair for car *(car seats)*, you know? And other things.

How did you start to work here?

My friend from Surin tell me to come to the bar and work. She say I can meet a lot of *farang* men, and make a lot of money. You know, I live in Surin, I live on a farm, not town, and I only see *farang* not many time before. But I see on TV and video *(laughing)*.

How about your family?

My parents, they work on the farm. I have one brother younger, he is 14, he go to school and help on the farm. My young sister has come now to work here in Pattaya. She work at different bar; same kind of bar, but she is only cashier. She not go with men. I hope she stay working a cashier, but she want to do what I do, I understand. She make about 3,000 baht for month for salary, and live in room at the bar.

Do you live with her?

I have room at this bar. I share room and bed with one girl. I stay here free, the room cost nothing.

What is it like to work here?

Here at ---- we are special bar. Upstairs men can get suck or fuck. I can do both. When first I start I cry after every time with man. But now, for me it is only work. No, it is not sex. I only think about the money, for parents and brother and my baby.

You have a baby? Can you tell me about your baby?

Yes, I am only 20, I have baby; daughter. She is four years old. Next year she will go to school and I want her to go so she can get good job someday, not same like me *(smiling)*. I need to pay her school; about 1,000 baht every month. I miss everyone at home. My sister and I talk much about our family. Sometime we cry, sometime we laugh. I miss my daughter the most. She stay with my parents. I have book of pictures of her and I look everyday. She is the number one in my life. Everything here I do for her.

So you are working like this for your family?

Yes. I want to work here maybe one more year and save money to go home and take care of my family. My brother he can go to school and learn how to fix motorcycles and cars, but I need to give the money to go. I want to go to school too – to learn English and maybe computer school. *Mamasan* is good person. She always tell me to put money in bank, save it, be careful, and not be like some girls and go drink and dance every night and spend money.

How much money do you make here?

Here I make good money. Sometime 1,000 baht for one day, and if a man pay the bar fine for me, I make more, sure. One time last month I made 7,000 baht. In one day! I remember I tell *mamasan* "Oh, I never have this much money in my life before." She laugh.

And how much did you make at your job in Surin?

How much I make for salary? One month I can make 4,000 baht. I work six days in one week, 12 hours in every day. I was 17 years old, I leave my school because I have baby and I try to find job [to] pay for me [so I can] take care of everyone. So I can not make enough to pay everything for my baby and family.

How many girls work here?

Not sure. Sometimes we have more than ten. Many girls come to work here, but cannot work like this. So they go home, or to work dancing.

Why don't you work in a go-go bar, or beer bar?

(*She thinks for a moment, as if the thought never occurred to her*) I cannot be a dancer – I am too shy. And a beer bar – I don't know. It is okay here. I like my friends here.

You mean the other girls?

Yes, I like other girls. We take care each other. Some girls have boyfriends – *farang* – but they always lie. Yes, the *farang* lie. They say "Oh, I love you, I not want you to work here." But do they pay the money so the girl not have to work? Never. They tell girl "I come back, take you [to] England, or America." They maybe come back. But I never see one customer take a girl home. Maybe go to an island, or Phuket for a week, only. But the girl she want to believe them, want to think can leave here sometime. Okay. But I don't listen when a man tell me that. How can I be sure? I have only work here ten months, but I hear stories, and see girls cry when they not get a letter, or get a letter tell them not to write or call some more. Why I want to do that?

So you do not have a boyfriend?

Right now I do not have boyfriend. Before I had Thai husband, but he hit me a lot. So I had to leave him. I leave him many time, but now I never want to be with him anymore. He come here one time to look for me, but *Mamasan* and other girls tell him go away or they call police. I think he was afraid of *Mamasan* more than police. She is bigger than he is *(laughing)*.

What do you do for fun?

Many other girls go out to disco every night, drink, dance, have a good time. They can try and forget about what the job here is. But they never have money after. So I stay here at night, just go to sleep in my room. But if a customer take me to hotel, I go there. Many times that is nice. If a big hotel with bathtub and hot water, cable TV and minibar I have a good time. Sometimes I can go swimming the next day. I love the time swimming. I can forget everything in the water. I think about before I was little and happy. Sometimes, when I have customer when I come to work and I get a good tip, I pay bar fine for me, and go to swimming somewhere, relax, then come back for work again.

What do you want in the future? Do you think about ten years from now?

Ten years? I cannot think about that. I think about now, how much money can I make. Make more money, save more money. Then I can go home to Surin to be with my family.

Is there anything you want to say about yourself for the people who will read this book?

What I want to tell people about me? I am girl who like people. I like many of the customer; but they are customer, not boyfriend. Some men they tell me, "You are beautiful, but you have cold heart." No, my heart is cold when I am working. And if I am with a man I am always working. So how can they know my other heart? I have a man who come last week. He want to talk, not go upstairs. He just want to sit and drink, he tip me 200 baht just for talk with him. If all men was like that, okay, I have very good job (*laughing*). Another man he pay the bar fine, take me to hotel. He do not want to fuck, he only want to talk, and sleep with me. In the morning he give me 2,000 baht. (*Smiling*) I like man like that. Who can know, maybe one day a man like that will want to be my boyfriend, and will not lie (*laughing again*). But I don't think so. Why not? Would you want a girl like me for girlfriend? You know what I do for work. I think I go back to Surin. If I go home Surin, maybe I will never have husband. Okay, no problem. I can be happy when I go back and take care of my baby and my family. That is what I want. To be happy.

18

DA: "JUST A CUSTOMER"

Da works in a beer bar in Pattaya. I met her in the early afternoon when she was on her way to work. She has to be at the bar from 3:00pm to 3:00am, with two days off a month. If she needs or wants more time off, she must pay the bar 200 baht per day missed. Da is tall, has a thin dark face and long black hair with a white streak down the side.

Q: Hi Da, thanks for talking to me, Can you tell me about yourself? Where are you from, how old are you?

Da: I come from small town near Korat, in Isaan, northeast Thailand. I am 22 year old. I work at ---- Bar for about six months. Before here I work massage shop over there for about one year.

How did you come to Pattaya?

I come here because my friend tell me come and make good money and meet foreign man. I come here because my family is poor and I cannot help them in my town. I must come here to make money to give to them.

Friends from your hometown told you this?

Yes, some friend of mine come to Pattaya before because other friend work here. My friend tell me easy to make money here and not work too much. Not like work at home. Must work in farm or shop, make little money. Or go to Bangkok work in factory or maid. Same, little money. So I come here.

And where do you live – at the bar or do you have a room somewhere else?

Before I stay [in] North Pattaya in house with other girl from massage. How many? Five girl together. Have one small house – two room, cooking room, toilet. Everyone pay 500 baht. But must pay motorcycle to go work, come home. So now I stay big room near bar. Have three girl stay together. Pay about 600 baht every month each girl. But can walk to work at bar, so is okay. And can go shopping or beach if wake up early.

And what do you think about the work?

It is okay. It is my job. I sit and talk with foreign man, ask him to buy me drink and pay bar. I talk with other girl, play card, watch movie on TV.

Can you decide whether to go with a man or not go with a man?

(*She gives a quizzical look*)…No, I don't think so. If man want to take me, okay I go.

But what if you don't like the man?

Some I like, some I do not like. But I go. It is my work. If I like the man I want him to take me, I ask him. Sometime say yes, sometime say no.

And what do you think about the sex? Does it bother you to have sex with men you don't know?

The first times, it didn't make me feel good, but it was my job at massage. Man like to have massage and finish. Okay. I can do for tip.

Do you ever like being with the customer?

Do I like to be with customer? For sex? No. But sometime not take a long time, take about 20 minutes. Not so bad. If take more than one hour, I tell man you have to finish or pay more. How much? I want 1,000 baht for short time. 2,000 for long time. I don't like to go long time. Why? Must to have sex two, three times. After do sex I want go home, sleep.

How much money do you make every month?

From bar salary about 7,000 baht if work every day and have customer buy drink.

And from going out with customers?

Sometime good, maybe 20,000 baht. Sometime small money, maybe 10,000 baht – low season.

What do you think about the customers?

I do not think about them. They do what they do. I understand, he want to have fun. Okay. Have fun. I tell them "Oh, you handsome. I like you." Sure, sometime true – have a handsome man. And nice man. But is just customer.

Do you ever think you will meet a man here who will take care of you so you don't have to do this anymore?

Maybe. But many girl have problem with foreign man. Go from bar maybe one year, come back to work again. Man is always no good. Have another lady. Tell girl he boring *(he's bored)*. So I think I do this work so I can save money and open shop in one year, two years.

So what about the future? What would you like to do?

In the future I will like to open a business about beauty shop. For the lady who work here. Stop going with man, and have the shop to help the lady here. Make-up, hair, nail. Make more money, then go home when I am 30 year old.

Is there anything you want to tell people who will read this book about the bar girls? About your life?

I want to ask why you like the lady here? Many lady here not understand. For sex? For me, for girl here, sex is what we do. Not fun for us. Drink, go out, is fun for us. So bring us to drink and go out, then we can have fun with sex, if enjoy to be with you.

UPDATE: Sadly, I heard that Da was killed in a motorcycle accident about a month after I spoke with her. She was on the back of the motorcycle with two other girls. They were heading home at around 5:00am from an after-work party at a disco, when their bike was hit by a truck. The two other girls were only slightly hurt, but Da did not survive.

19

DAI: "I THINK I AM HAPPY"

Dai is tall and slim, with long black hair and very light skin. I met up with her in the lobby of a four-star hotel, outside of an upscale pub/disco. This is where Dai meets her customers, or "friends" as she calls them. Impeccably dressed in a designer dress and shoes, with tastefully put on make-up, Dai could be out for a night in New York City or Los Angeles.

Q: Hello Dai, can you tell me about yourself; your family, where you come from?

Dai: Sure, I come from Petchburi, south of Bangkok. I have a nice family, they don't know I do this – come out at night to meet men. I have a job also. In office, I cannot say where. But it is a good job with a good company. No one there know I do this.

Why do you keep it a secret from your family and friends? Is it so bad?

(Thinking)…Well, I don't think it is a bad thing to do *(laughing)*. But other people do think it is a bad thing. The people [who] work in my office are nice. Have family, go work, go home, go temple. I never hear them talk about going to a bar. Go to restaurant for enjoy, but never some place like this. If I see someone from office here I think I will die. *(Laughing)* My family cannot understand something like this.

So why do you do it?

I like to come here to meet someone sometime. And I like to listen to the music and dance and have good time. And sometime meet some nice man. If I like him I will go with him if he like me. Yes, he must give me money. How much? More than 3,000 baht. I ask for 5,000 or 6,000. For one night, yes. I take very good care man. They always want my phone number. *(Laughing)* I can do anything they want. Want another girl, sure no problem, if I like the girl. But more money. Maybe 7,000 baht for me, other girl I don't care. Sometime it with wife or girlfriend. If they pay I don't care.

So you do it for the money?

The money can buy me some things I like. New clothes, dresses, shoe. *(Smiling)* And I live [in a] very nice condo. Cannot pay for this with salary from job.

But *(she stops talking for a moment)*…I like to go out and I like to have sex with men.

So why not get a boyfriend?

(Laughing) This is fun more. I am 34 year old. When I am young girl I am told Thai lady should not like sex. Maybe different now, what they say to a Thai lady 20 year old. But I am not polite if I like sex with different man. So I do not tell any friend before. I have some friend here, Thai lady, we can talk about this. But not my family, not people in office. So I can come here and enjoy and if I meet man I can have sex and get money. That's good for me, yes?

So how often do you come here?

I come this place about two times in a week. Saturday I go [to] a different bar.

And how many nights do you meet a man and go with him?

If I can, every time! If I don't meet someone I like or he don't have money for me, I go [to a] different disco or come back again. I don't worry – I meet a lot of man.

Do you use a condom? Worry about meeting someone who is dangerous?

The man go with me always use condom. No condom, no sex. Always. I never have a problem with man. I talk to the man before I go with them. If I think not nice man, I don't go with him.

Are you happy with your life the way it is?

(Thinking)…Yes, I think so. I enjoy. I enjoy my work in office. I enjoy this. I enjoy to spend money. So, I think I am happy.

UPDATE: I called Dai to see how she was doing. She said she had met a man she liked who was going to bring her to Europe, but the plan had hit a snag. Since she was going to have to leave her office job, Dai wanted him to give her a sum of money to keep in the bank in Thailand in case things didn't work out. She said he was not happy with that idea, so it looked like the plan for Europe would not go forward.

I asked Dai if she was upset:

Dai: No. If he does not want to give me that money, we would have a problem sometime. If he is cheap now, what will happen in Europe? So I will stay in Thailand. Maybe some day I will meet a more nice man.

20

EET: "A GUY WHO LIKE TO SPEND MONEY DO NOT BUY A CHEAP WATCH"

I was introduced to Eet by Dai. Eet is short and slim. She has dark skin and has dyed her long hair a dark blonde. Her English is fluent and the entire interview was conducted through English. I met Eet in a coffee shop in an upscale shopping mall, where she says she "spends a lot of time and money". She is wearing designer shoes and jeans, and a tight Porsche ("my last boyfriend had one") t-shirt. She orders a latte and a chocolate chip cookie.

Q: What can you tell me about yourself Eet; where are you from, how old are you?

Eet: Well, I'm 33 years old. I'm from the north of Thailand – Chiang Mai, but I came to Bangkok when I was 18 to go to university. I went to a big university here for about a year, met a rich Thai guy and quit. We partied for about a year, then I met a guy from France and I left the Thai guy. I have a 10-year-old son from the French guy.

146

Where is your son, with the father?

No, my son is with my older sister in Chiang Mai. Actually I haven't seen him in about seven years. My son I mean. I haven't seen the father in about nine years. I don't even know where he is.

Why haven't you seen your son in so long?

My sister is a good mother for him. He's a good boy. He does well in school. I miss him, but my sister is a better mother than me *(shrugs)*. So I am happy for both of them.

What happened with the father?

We broke up. He went back to France.

What were you doing when you were with him? Did you ever go back to school?

No, I never had to go back. I never had to work with either my Thai boyfriend or him. Don't laugh at me please – but I have never had a job. I had a shop before, but I never work in anyplace.

How have you been able to do that?

(Laughing) Rich boyfriends. I have been to France with that boyfriend. After him I met a guy from South Africa. He made jewellery – gold – and he was rich. I went to South Africa with him two or three times. I didn't like it though. Then after him I had a German boyfriend. I was with him for four years. He had a

business in Germany. I lived there for almost one year with him. We travelled to Austria and Switzerland and Italy. I liked the mountains. The snow.

And what happened with him?

His business was family business. A factory. His father died and he had to work all the time at the factory. It was near Frankfurt. I didn't like it there and wanted to move in Germany or come back to Thailand. He couldn't leave there so I came back to Thailand. But we are still friends. He understood the reason. So he gave me money and I started my business. Then last year I sold it.

Where did you learn your English? It's excellent.

I started to learn English in high school. I was good at it. And I studied more in uni *(university)*. My French boyfriend spoke good English and I couldn't speak French so I spoke a lot of English with him. And watched movies, TV. The guy from South Africa spoke English, too. The German guy didn't, so I learned to speak German okay when I was there. So I can speak three languages. Good, huh?

Very good. You could probably get a very good job, since you are able to speak Thai, English and German.

Sure, I think so. But I don't want to work in office

or for hotel. I like coming to meet men.

So how long have you been coming to the discos and meeting men?

For a long time. That is how I met my German boyfriend. Of course I stopped when I was with him, but I have been doing it even when I had my shop.

And why do you do it – you go to bars and meet men, and they pay you for sex, right?

Yes. I like this life. I go out to party when I want, usually I can choose if I want to go with a man; I can sleep late and go shopping. For me it's a good life.

But how long can you do this life?

I'm not old. Look at me, I don't think I look old. Do I look like a cheap bar girl? I don't think so. So I think I can do this for maybe five more years. Or maybe I meet another rich guy and I stay with him.

So what type of men do you look for when you go to the bars?

I like tourist. So if I see a guy I might like, I smile at them. Or if I don't see anyone, if someone smiles at me I go talk to them. Ask them where they are from, what do they do. Look at their clothes, and their watch. A guy who like to spend money do not buy a cheap watch.

So why tourists?

They pay more *(smiling)*. Guys who live here don't like to pay so much.

How much is that?

Five or six thousand baht for one night. Is that a lot? I don't think so. I know what girls get in Europe. And I'm worth it. I can make a guy very happy *(laughing)*.

And how much can you make in a month? *(The average salary for an office worker is 12,000–15,000 baht a month; 20,000 would be a very good salary).*

I make 60,000 baht a month, sometimes more. And the guys take me shopping, too. It's more than just money.

Do you ever feel bad about what you do?

Why? It is what I do. I have a good life. I enjoy going out with my friends, dancing, shopping. I have travelled, I will travel again. Maybe Italy, Brazil, Hawaii. I could not do that working in a mall.

And in the future, is that what you see for yourself?

I will be okay. I will open a new business or marry a rich guy. I do not worry *(smiling)*.

UPDATE:

Eet: No rich guy yet, but not worried. Some man buy me a gold chain before, cost about 25,000 baht, so I am happy. Very happy.

21

WAN: "MY LIFE IS MY LIFE"

Wan is thin and tall – very tall for a Thai woman. At 177 cm (or 5'9"), Wan stands out in a crowd, figuratively and literally. I was put in touch with Wan by a friend of hers who had heard about my project and thought I should hear Wan's story. We met in an upscale mall and sat down to have a coffee with her. Wan has a pretty face and long, straight black hair parted in the middle. She would pass for a bank teller or executive secretary were she to dress in business attire. Instead, she is in a blue Chelsea FC t-shirt, blue jeans and Keds sneakers: making her appear to be in her early 20s, not early 30s. She has big brown eyes, a big smile and an infectious laugh that also draws attention. All this contradicts the story that Wan told me. Wan just started talking and didn't stop until the end.

Q: Hi Wan, can you tell me about yourself? Where you are from, how and why you are talking to me?

Wan: Well, a friend of mine told me you were writing a book about women in Thailand and thought my story would be good for you, so here I am. I am 31 years old, I come from a village near the border with Burma, in the western part of Thailand. My village is poor, I had three brothers and two sisters; I am the second youngest, just one sister is younger than me. My parents raised vegetables that they sold in the market – corn, carrots, tomatoes. We lived in a small house, everyone together, and I was a happy little girl, I remember that. Then when I was 11 or 12, I was told I could not go to school anymore, and that make me very sad. My family did not have enough money for all the children to go to school. My oldest brother just finished high school and was going to a technical school and it was more important for him for that, so I had to stop and work in the farm with my parents. I was very unhappy. I could not see my friends. Well, I could see them, they went to school everyday while I worked in the farm. But it was how it was – I had to work to help the family *(smiles)*. I am not angry now, but I was then.

When I was about 13 years old I was raped. By a friend of my brother. He told me he would hurt me if I told anyone, so I didn't. But I was never the same from after that happened. I was very sad but I couldn't tell anyone and no one knew what was wrong with me. My father would yell at me for being sad. So when I was 14 years old I went to Rachaburi, which is a big city a little far from my village and a little far from Bangkok. I got a job selling things in the market and met a boy who was 16. I wanted to be grown up so we decided to get married. I went back home with this boy when I became 15 and we were married in my village. He got a job in Bangkok as [a] construction [worker] and I went to Bangkok with him. We got a room and he worked construction and I helped people in our street. I iron clothes for the laundry woman and wash dishes for the food cart woman and sew something for another woman. I thought that my life would be okay.

Then the police take my husband one day, put him in the jail. They said he selling drugs to the people he working with. I don't know. He tell me [he did] not, and we don't have money. But he go to jail for a long time. Five years. I go back to my village but I cannot stay there. I cannot work on the farm again. So I go back to Bangkok, I know a girl – she work in a karaoke bar. I get a job for service – waitress. I am 15 year old.

One day the owner tell me I cannot work anymore, too young. I say what will I do? One girl there she tell me "Come on, we go to Pattaya." I say, "I don't think so, what will I do?" She tell me she will take care [of] me. So I go. Oh, and I get divorce from husband. Is easy to do because I am young and he in prison, so my father, he pay in my village and I divorce.

So I am [a] 15-year-old and in Pattaya. I get job cleaning in hotel. My friend she go to work in body massage. She make good money, I do not. One day I tell her I want to work in massage. I have to get paper say that I am 19 year old, it no problem and I start work in massage. I make a lot of money (*smiles*). I am tall and with make-up I look like older.

Then one day I meet a guy come in for massage. He from America – about 22 year old – from Florida. He take good care of me – give me money for family, when he go home he give me money to live and I don't have to work massage anymore. When he come back to Thailand I am 18 year old and we get married. He take me back to Florida. At first I like. He live in a big house. His family really love me. I stay there two year. But after two year I am sad. I miss Thailand. I cannot speak good English. I don't know any Thai people. I am very young. He was a good man, I still talk to him today and many time I am very sorry to hurt him. I ask him is okay for me to go back to Thailand to see my family and he say yes. But I don't tell him I will not come back to Florida. He come to Thailand to try and have me come back, but I cannot. He cry, I cry, but I know I cannot go back to stay there anymore. So again I get divorce. I am 22 year old and I am marry and divorce two time already! *(Laughs quickly)*

So now what can I do? I go to work in bar in Bangkok and Pattaya. I go with many men, I send money to family to help them. I have my oldest brother he has a good job, but two other brother no good. Lazy. Just drink and do nothing. And my sisters, one is okay and the other one is lazy like my brothers. My father and mother get older and cannot work farm anymore. My lazy brothers and sister don't do anything and the farm just gone. So my good brother and me we pay and pay so my parent can keep house. I must work bar in Bangkok and Pattaya, many year I work. You know how many man I go with? So many I will never know. Then one time I meet a guy from Canada and he really like me, I think he is good man, and he take me to Canada. So now I have been Canada for more than three year. We marry in Canada. Sometime it is good, sometime I miss Thailand. In Canada I learn about jewellery business and I have good job to clean jewellery. I make good salary, I have some Thai friend there.

My husband is good man. I come back about one month ago because my oldest brother he die in accident. His truck have accident and I don't know, he die. So I come back but will go back Canada next month. I love my parent. My brothers no good, my one sister not good. I take care their kids for them when I am here. What happen when I go, I don't know. I always send money to family, my husband not understand, he say "They don't help you before, why you do for them?" I say "Because they are my family." He is not Thai, he don't understand. Am I happy now in Canada with my life? I think so. I want to have baby, but my husband don't want. He have a son already 16 from before. I think I will be a good mother, I want to have a daughter that I can take care and give a good life to. Then I will be happy.

So, when you look at your life, how do you see yourself? How do you feel about the men you have met, the way your life has turned out?

My life is my life. It has happened. I cannot change it, I have been with many men and now I have one. He is a good man, he is more than 20 year older than me. I will take care of him.

One more question: do you regret anything, would you have done anything different in your life if you could?

Sometimes I wish I tell my brothers about the boy

who rape me. I see him in my village when I go home. I hate him. I had many dream when I was young about my brothers kill him, and in the dream I was very happy. But now…*(shrugs her shoulders)* I think now maybe I should ask my husband before if we can have a baby. Yeah, this husband, ask before we marry. That is what I want. My baby to take care of, to make sure she is happy and go to school and have a good mother that she will tell she loves very much.

UPDATE: Wan contacted me by email from Canada. She has decided she will leave her husband and return to Thailand. She said that her husband told her again that he does not want to have another child. She said that she has admitted to herself that she is not happy in Canada. She does not want to go through another Canadian winter and misses Thailand, her family, her friends and Thai food. Wan does not know what she will do for work when she comes back to Thailand.

22

Fim and Sweet: "Come on and party"

I found Fim and Sweet drinking together at a large dance club in Pattaya. I introduced myself and asked if they would be willing to talk to me. We agreed to meet the following day at 3:00pm. They showed up just after 4:00pm.

Q: Hi Fim and Sweet, thanks for coming out to talk with me. I explained a little about what I am doing – the book – last night, do you have any questions?

Fim: No, you want to know about our life.

Sweet: And you pay us for our talk?

Yes, I want to know about your life, and yes, I will pay you. Can you tell me about yourselves? How old are you, where you are from?

Sweet: I am 22 year old, we both come from Mukdahan. Have you heard of that place?

It is a small city in Isaan, across the Mekong River from Laos, right?

Fim: Oh, very good! Yes, that is right. We come from there. And I am also 22 year old.

Sweet, how did you get your nickname? It's not Thai.

Sweet: I have another friend name "Wan" – and that is mean "sweet" in Thai. So I am also Sweet, but now we have different name.

Okay, that's a good idea. Can you tell me what you are doing in Pattaya? Do you work in a bar?

Fim: No, when we come here we not old enough to work bar, we are only 19. So we go to beach or to disco to meet customer.

So you don't work for anyone, you stand along the beach or go to clubs?

Sweet: We don't go to beach now. Those lady on the beach are *ee-gaa-lee (this is the most derogatory form of the Thai word for prostitute, the closest equivalent to "street whore")*.

Fim: Yes, we go to the disco and dance and drink and meet a man, not sell on street.

Interesting. In English we say we "look down on" someone. Do you look down on the women on the beach?

Fim: Yes. They cannot work in bar, cannot dance, not have money for disco, must stay on the beach and go with any man.

Sweet: We do not do that.

But you said you did that when you got here – how long did you work on the beach?

Fim: Not long time. Maybe two, three week. We get card say we are 20 year old so we can go to disco.

Okay, and when you came here three years ago from Mukdahan, what was your plan? To work selling sex?

Fim: Yes. And to have a party.

Sweet: Yes. Mukdahan have nothing to do, we are boring *(bored)* so we come to Pattaya to have fun and meet men and make money.

Did you work or go to school in Mukdahan? And what about your families, do they know what you are doing here?

Fim: No, my family think I work in restaurant in Chonburi *(Chonburi is the capital city of the province where Pattaya is located)*. In Mukdahan I work restaurant my aunt. My salary is so low, maybe 3,000 baht in one month. What can I do with that?

Sweet: I don't work in Mukdahan. I learn about beauty shop before. Cut hair, paint nail, face massage. But no have work. So I tell my family I work beauty shop in Chonburi.

What are your families like? What would they think if they found out what you were really doing?

Sweet: I have my mother and father and one sister, she is 16 year old. And uncle, aunt and grandparents.

Fim: I have mother and father and three brother. I am the baby (*laughing*). I think they would be sad if they know I work like this.

And Sweet, what would your family think?

Sweet: The same. Sad.

So you came to Pattaya and knew that this is what you would be doing? If your families would be sad, what does that make you feel about it?

Sweet: It is my life. I cannot stay in Mukdahan. When I am 18 years old I want to come Pattaya and enjoy.

Fim: The same. We come here to have a good time and make a lot of money (*laughing*).

Where do you live?

Fim: We stay in a room near the Soi Buakaew Market.

You stay together? And what is the room like, how much is it every month?

Sweet: Yes, we stay together. The room is a room, small. Have shower and toilet. Rent we pay 2,500 baht for one month.

Can you tell me what your average day is like? What time do you wake up and what do you do during the day?

Fim: We wake up two o'clock or three o'clock in afternoon. Take shower, go out for eating.

Sweet: Maybe go to mall, maybe we meet some man.

You go to the mall to try and meet customers?

Sweet: Yes, why not? Sometime we meet, sometime no.

Fim: If no we can go eat more or maybe go to movie if have money.

Sweet: Or go home, sleep, watch TV. Go out to disco 11 o'clock.

And at the mall, how do you meet customers there?

Sweet: We wait outside or inside, sit and smile at man. If they smile we say hello, where you go?

Fim: We talk to them, ask if want to go to room. Easy to find customer there.

You keep saying "we". Do you both go or just one of you?

Fim: Up to man. Can take both if want, no problem.

Sweet: Yes, no problem for me.

And how much do you charge to go with a man from the mall?

Fim: *(Shrugging)* Up to man. More than 700 baht. Maybe 1,000.

For each of you?

162

Sweet: *(Looking shocked)* Of course!

How long will you stay with a man for that much?

Fim: Until he finish. Maybe one hour, maybe 20 minute.

How many times a week do you go to the mall and how many of those times do you think you find a man?

Sweet: *(Thinking)* We go about three time one week. And I think every time we can find a man.

Fim: If like now, tourist season. If low season maybe not so many foreigner.

What do you do with the money, do you save it?

Sweet: *(Laughing)* Shopping! Buy make-up, maybe some shoe or jeans.

Fim: Keep for evening, so can buy one drink at disco.

And do you charge the men the same at the disco?

Fim: No, at disco have to pay 1,500 short time and 2,500 long time.

What is the difference between finding a customer at the mall and finding one at a disco?

Sweet: At mall is short time, and we are not beautiful like at disco. *(Laughing)*

Okay so you arrive at the disco at 11:00pm – do you want to find customers right away?

Fim: No, like to dance, customer buy us drink. We

want to have fun and party.

Sweet: But if want to go short time, can. But must come back to disco. We don't want to go home, we want to stay out and have a party.

So you stay out at the disco, sounds like you like to drink?

Fim: Yes, sure. And smoke ganja. *(Laughing)*

Any other drugs?

Sweet: No, no good. But if someone give ecstasy, can do. *(Fim nods in agreement)*

Do you like the sex with the customers?

Fim: Sometime. If feeling good, yes.

Sweet: If he is fun man, sure.

Do you mean if he is in a good mood?

Sweet: Yes, if he buy us drink, have good time, laughing. Sex is party, too.

Fim: Yes, if have good heart, not *kee-nee-aow (cheap)*.

So it doesn't bother you to sell sex? You don't want boyfriends or husbands, children?

Sweet: No, if want to do that can stay Mudkahan.

Fim: For me it is no problem to sell sex. Can get money, maybe go shopping with man for phone, clothes. I cannot get these things if I stay home.

And what about your future? How long do you think

you will do this?

Fim: I don't know, I think maybe two, three year more. Then maybe I will be tired and go home.

Sweet: Or maybe meet some nice man and get married, have children.

So you both want a normal life someday? You don't think living like this will spoil that for you?

Sweet: No, why? This is me now, I am young. I want to have fun. Later I will be serious. *(Fim is nodding next to her).*

And what about HIV/AIDS or other disease? Do you use condoms?

Fim: Yes, every time.

Sweet: But for some customer I know, no have to use condom.

Is that the same for you, Fim? If you know the man do you trust him?

Fim: No, I use condom every time. *(Sweet shrugs)*

How much do you make in one month?

Fim: Sometime make 25,000 baht one month, sometime 30,000, If very slow, maybe 15,000, but not less.

Sweet: Yes, about the same. And I have more than my friend in Mukdahan.

Okay, is there anything else either of you would like to

say? **We hope a lot of people will read the book.**

Fim: *(Laughing)* Come on and party in Pattaya!

Sweet: Yes, we want to meet some man more! *(Laughing)* We have a good party here.

UPDATE: A few weeks after the interview, my translator informed us that she was at the mall and ran into Fim, walking alone. She asked where Sweet was and Fim told her that a customer had reported Sweet to the police for stealing his ATM card, cash and mobile phone, so Sweet had gone back to Mukdahan to stay for awhile. When asked if the report of the theft was true, Fim shrugged her shoulders and replied "Maybe. Sometime that happen," and then walked away, saying that she didn't want to say anything more.

23

SINE: "I HOPE I AM HAPPY AGAIN"

I met Sine at a street-side restaurant near Soi Cowboy, a one block strip of go-go and beer bars in downtown Bangkok. Sine is a "hostess" at one of Soi Cowboy's go-go bars, and was introduced to me by one of the bar's dancers whom I had interviewed. She is tall and thin, with shoulder-length hair. She has yet to change into her uniform for work, a low-cut evening gown. Her English was excellent, my translator was only needed twice during the interview.

Q: Hello Sine, nice to meet you, thank you for talking with me. I'm talking to many women who work in the bars; I want to find out about their lives, so thank you for helping me. Can you tell me a little about yourself? Where do you come from, how old you are, where you live?

Sine: Nice to meet you, too. My name is Sine, but that is my name only from when I was nine year old, before name Pui. I am now 31 years old, and now I live in Bangkok.

Are you from Bangkok?

No. I grow up in Isaan, near city of Buriram, but not in the city. In a village abut 20 kilometre from there.

Can you tell me about growing up there, and how you got to Bangkok?

I not remember being happy. Maybe sometime I was happy, but in my house was not good. When I was little I was fat. I know now I am not, but when I was small I was. My nickname was Pui – that is for *poom pui* – "fat" in Thai language. So my father and my brother don't like me. They *lawr len* (*tease*) me. And my father and brother call me stupid. They hit me, kick me. My brother tell me I am like dog.

That is shocking. What about your mother? Or other people, didn't anyone try to help you?

My mother go away when I was very young, maybe two year old. Where did she go? I not know. Now I not know what happen, I think I will never know. Not have anyone to help me. I have to do everything from when I am so small, maybe five year old. Clean, cook food, wash the clothes. I don't go to school. And everyday my father and brother they hit me if I am not good. And call me the name – fat, stupid. I cry every day and every night.

(Sine is very calm and matter-of-fact as she is telling her story, so I ask her about that) **Sine, does it upset you to remember, or to talk about this?**

I am okay. This was a long time ago, many things happen after this time. When I am about nine year old my friend who live in the village say she will go to Bangkok to live with her mother. I cry and tell her "Please take me with you". This is another girl, same age as me. One night my brother and father are drinking and my friend come and say, "Come on". I go with her and her mother take me with them on a bus. I take nothing from my house, but I am excited and scared, too. They tell me I will live in Bangkok. I am so happy to be away, not stay with my father and brother. Before I not know what happen, but now I know. My friend mother, she call to my father and say "Pui stay with me now," and my father say he don't care.

You were lucky to have a good friend and her mother – but isn't what they did like kidnapping?

But my father he say he don't care. He even send the paper for me to go to school in Bangkok. So I start my new life. I tried to go to school but I was not smart like other students because I didn't go to school in the village. I like school because I have friend there, but I cannot read and write so good, other students not so nice for me. But one teacher is very nice for me, she help me to learn to read and write and in maybe one year more I am the same as other student. And she want me to change nickname to Sine, so I can forget Pui.

And so you stayed with your friend and her mother until you finished school?

Yes. I stay with them, go to school. I finish in high school. Oh, and when I am about 15 year old I change. I get tall *(laughing)*. Before I was short and fat, then I get tall. And I play sport; basketball and volleyball, so not fat no more! After high school I am 172 centimetre, now I am 174 *(approximately 5'7")*.

Did you ever talk to or see your father during this time? Tell him how well you were doing?

No. I not want to see him. I am afraid he will make me come back. And my new mother she take care [of] me, she is better for me.

She really changed your life – do you still see her or your friend?

They move to America. My new mother she meet American man and he take them there. I cannot go because cannot have visa – I am not her daughter. When they go I miss [them] too much. I can talk to them still now, but what can I tell them, that I am bar lady? I don't want to say that, so we talk now not so much.

It sounds like your life was going well. You finished high school, and even though your friend went to the U.S., you had a new life, right?

But I have no money to go university. I have to work. So I get job in department store. I make salary okay, have a quiet life. I think I will meet someone some day and marry and have family.

What happened?

When I am about 20 year old, I continue work in department store. I meet a man from Australia, he come in store. He like me, I like him. He is first one to tell me I am beautiful and I believe because he take care [of] me. He 22 year old. He stay in Thailand sometime, maybe one month, two month, go and work in Australia, send me money, tell me to study English. After maybe two year he come to live in Thailand. He work about writing for magazine. We live together eight year. We have one son, now he is six year old. Maybe I am stupid because I never go to school to learn something more. My boyfriend he tell me he can pay for school, more English or computer. But I don't go, I want to take care [of] my son. Then about two year ago my boyfriend he go away, home to Australia he said. I

171

miss him very much. He send money sometime, but then he say he cannot anymore. Who can take care [of] my son? I must work something. I work department store again, but money is not enough. I know about Soi Cowboy from my boyfriend and his friend. I see before. Foreigner like to come here, look at the lady in bar. One night I come to here and talk to lady outside, ask how much salary, what about foreign man? Salary is more. Can have sex with man for money, can get 20,000, 30,000 baht every month.

But there must be other things you can do? You have excellent English. You have been through a lot and I'm not judging you, but it seems like you gave up quickly.

(Sine thinks for a moment, then shrugs her shoulders) I need to take care [of] my son. Where is boyfriend? He leave us, so now I do this. Sometime I see his friend, they see me here. Now he know this is what happen when leave mother and son alone.

Okay, so what do you do exactly? What is your job?

I am hostess. I stand outside the bar, go-go bar, and tell customer to come inside. Maybe ask them to buy drink for me.

And sometimes you go out with the customers?

Yes, of course. If it is nice man, I think no problem. We can go short time. Have room here on soi.

And what do you ask the man to pay?

He must pay bar 600 baht. And for me 2,000 baht. I stay with him two hour, maybe three if nice man.

Never more than that? You never spend the night?

No. Cannot. Have to go and see my son before he go to school.

And what do you think about what you do?

(Again, Sine shrugs as she answers) I not think anything. It is my job. I go with a man, he have sex, he pay.

You just said, "he has sex." Obviously you do too, but do you not see it that way?

For me, okay, it is sex, too. But it is my job to do that, I don't think about it.

And do you have safe sex all the time?

Yes, no condom, no sex. If man just want with the hand okay, but for suck and sex, must have condom.

Do you think you are taking good care of your son now?

Yes, I see him in the morning when go to school. Then I sleep. Then I meet him at school and I go to work.

Who takes care of him while you work?

Have a old woman live on *soi (street)*, she take care of some children because mother have to work. Have maybe eight or nine or ten children stay her home. It is good for my son I think, he have some friend, can play, watch TV.

And what about the future? How long do you think you will do this?

I know in the future I will not do this. I save some money, maybe I start a shop somewhere. Maybe I meet some man who take care of me again. If happen again I know I will go to some school and get smart. I hope someone will love me again, I am lonely and sad many times. But I love my son and will do everything for him. I want him to have a good life. So this is what I must do.

Well, thanks Sine, is there anything else you want to say?

Talk about what?

Anything; about you, your life, something to say to anyone who will read the book?

Make sure you take care [of] your children. This is not a life I want. But it is life I have. I have happy two times in my life. I hope I am happy again.

24

AER: "I AM OKAY; SOMETIME LONELY, SOMETIME SAD, SOMETIME HAPPY"

Aer has long dark hair that frames her thin face. She is wearing sandals, denim shorts and an oversized, bright orange t-shirt that says "Chicago Yankees" over a picture of an American football. She's asked me to meet her in a fast food restaurant in a shopping mall not far from the bar she works in. She is a waitress in a go-go bar on Soi Cowboy, and heard about me through her friend Sine.

Hi Aer, how are you? Thank you for talking with me. I think you know I would like to ask you some questions about your life. Can you tell me where you are from, how old you are, about your family?

Yes, I come from Surat Thani, I am 35 year old. I have one daughter 14 year old, but she stay with my mother in Surat Thani. *(Surat Thani is a city of 130,000, approximately 330 miles south of Bangkok).*

How long have you been in Bangkok?

175

This time I have been Bangkok about three year. First time I come I am 22 year old.

And why did you come to Bangkok the first time?

I come to work in the bar. I need money for my daughter and mother.

What were you doing in Surat Thani that you didn't make enough money to support them?

I work in small mini-store shop. Cashier. My friend work in Bangkok and she tell me I can come to there and make money more.

What was your salary at the shop?

My salary about 150 baht every day, I work about ten hour, 11 hour every day. My friend tell me I can make 1,000 baht and more in Bangkok every day.

Did you know what you would be doing and did that bother you at all?

Yes, a little. I know I will work in a bar. I think maybe I will have sex with customer – foreigner. But I think I will not do for so long. Maybe six month or one year.

So you came to Bangkok with your friend, and what happened?

She work waitress at go-go bar in Patpong. Was different then. Now is big market, have many many bars. I work waitress with my friend. Have salary 4,000 baht every month but can get money from drink if customer buy for me. And if go with customer can get bar fine money and money from customer.

So how much did you start to make?

At first I don't go with customer. I'm a little shy. But one guy have a friend want to take my friend, and he want to take me. So I go with him. I think bar fine about 400 baht, and he give me 1,500 baht. We stay all night with them in nice hotel.

What did you think after, about going with someone who paid for sex with you?

(Thinking, then shrugs) Was okay. Hard to remember now. I was different girl then.

How is that?

I think I only have to do for one year. I think everyone will be nice like that man. But I scare about the sex.

And now, what's different?

(Laughing) Many thing. I have been working like this for 13 year. I know everyone not so nice *(laughing again)*. And I not scare about sex.

What do you think about the sex?

I like it. I like sex. For me it is good. Not every time, but I like to do sex. So this is good job for me, true? *(Laughing)*

Better than not liking it. I've talked to many women who say they don't like it, they say they just do it for the money.

(Laughing) I not do for free. But I enjoy to be with a man. I only go with man I think I like. But that is now, before I go with many man I don't like.

Okay, so how many men did you go with when you started? And how much money do you think you were making?

Oh, long time ago. I go with maybe two or three customer in one week. I think money I make is about 20,000 baht for when I start. I am very happy.

So you thought you had made the right decision?

Yes, I thought working in the bar was good idea. Money is good, people are fun.

Did you go back to see your daughter and mother?

Sometime. On the holiday. Songkran, Mother Day, Loy Kratong. And [the] birthday [of] my daughter. 22 February.

Then what happened in your life? Did you start to dance or work in other kinds of bars?

I stay bar in Patpong about one year, always waitress. Then I go bar in Nana Plaza, work waitress there. Then I work bar beer in Pattaya, two or three year, come back to Bangkok. But I also go to Europe three time.

Tell me about going to Europe. Was it with a customer you met?

First time I work in Patpong bar some man ask me to come Austria, but I cannot. I have my daughter [and she] is only one year old. And I not know where Austria is. So I say no. But I meet a man at bar in Pattaya. I know him one week, I ask him can I come to Holland, he say "Okay". I am shock, but I go. We get passport and ticket and visa and I go Holland. I stay about three month.

What did you think of Holland?

Oh, very nice. People are nice. It is summer the first time, so weather is nice. I go back again to see this man around New Year and weather very cold. I only stay one month *(laughing)*.

So was this guy your boyfriend? How long did your relationship with him last and what happened in the end?

Yes, he boyfriend almost five year. I go Holland three time, one time is for more than one year. He come [to] Thailand. He send money for me so I don't work bar. I work bar but not go with customer. I think maybe someday we get marry. But he meet some Holland lady and leave me. I am very sad for long time.

So you went back to work?

Yes, what can I do?

Have you had any other boyfriends since that time?

(*Thinking*) No, not like that man. Have many regular customer, no boyfriend.

What makes someone a boyfriend and not a customer?

They take care [of the girl]. Give money for family and the girl not have to work in bar, maybe give money to have shop or go to school.

Not love?

That is love. If pay for everything, then that show love.

So after you split up with your Dutch boyfriend, what happened?

I work more in bar. I go Singapore and work.

Do you mean that you worked in bars in Singapore? For how long?

Yes, in the disco and hotel. I go three times. Stay two weeks, one week and one time more than six month. But that time was last time and I overstay visa and have to come back on bus. I very happy to see Thailand again.

Why did you go to Singapore? Do you make more money there?

Oh yes, can make a lot of money there. But a little

bit dangerous. How? Police try to catch Thai lady work at disco and hotel.

So how do Thai girls get to work there?

We can go to Singapore, get tourist visa. But immigration ask many question. "Why you come here? How long you stay? Where you stay? Where is your money?" If cannot show money and hotel, have to go back [to] Thailand.

So you get a tourist visa?

Yes, can get one-week or two-week visa. Then go to Geylang Street. Find many Thai girl, many Chinese girl, some Vietnam girl. And many customer. But many police, too. If police catch they take [you] to jail. And if not have aeroplane ticket to go home, you must stay jail maybe one week or two week, try have friend send money for ticket. If cannot, [you will] have problem. Police in the jail cut hair, sometime the *tom (closest translation would be "butch")* police lady slap the girl. Sometime take money. So not good to have police catch.

And you never got caught by the police?

No, never. But many time have to run away. Go to top of hotel and climb to next building, like a monkey *(laughing)*. One time I am running away from police lady with my friend and police lady grab her hair. But

181

my friend have, what do you call, wig? Yes, she have wig and policeman pull her hair and hair come off. We run away. Very funny. We go to disco and bar Orchard Tower, everyone know that place. If in disco must find someone to say "this my girlfriend" if police come in. Same shopping, better to go with some foreigner.

So to take that chance you must be able to make a lot of money.

Yes. Money can make a lot. For sex sometime can get 300 Singapore dollar *(equal to approximately 250USD or 7,500 Thai baht)*. For short time can get 150 or 200 Singapore dollar. Sometime have two customer, three customer one night. And in daytime can get five or six customer one day. But can get only 50 Singapore dollar. One day I have ten customer. Yes, can make good money.

You had sex with that many men in one day?

Yes. You think is a bad thing, yes? But I don't think that. I take care of my mother and my daughter and I take care myself. Sex is what I do. Maybe I cannot explain to someone. But I am a good person, I think. I do not hurt other people. I don't do something wrong with my money. No drugs, no gamble, no alcohol.

So you returned to Thailand and have been working in the sex business for how long now?

13 year.

And now? You're happy working in the bar?

It is okay. I am waitress. I can make money very good. I meet many people. I have friend like Sine. I have many customer.

What do you think about it all now – do you wish you had done something different with your life or are you okay with it?

Many time I think about if I don't start to work in a bar. What would my life be like today? Maybe I will find out in my next life *(smiling)*. I have choose to do this life. I am okay; sometime lonely, sometime sad, sometime happy.

And what about the future? What do you want to do?

(Thinking) Not sure. Now I work the bar, meet more customer. I hope my dream come true, that my daughter have a good life and is happy. And maybe my man in Holland come back to me.

UPDATE: I ran into Aer and Sine having dinner a few months after the interviews and asked them how things were going:

Aer: Yes, good. I have good man take care [of] me for two week. Pay bar, we go to see my daughter and mother together.

Sine *(smiling)*: Handsome man!

So, is this going to be a new boyfriend?

Aer: *(frowning)* I don't think so. Before I think so but now he go home to Europe already more than two week, he never call me. So I think no.

That's too bad. Did you like him?

Aer: Sure, he take care of me and daughter and mother. We have good time together. But now maybe finish. *Mai phen rai (This is a popular expression in Thai culture, here meaning "it doesn't matter" or "no big deal")*.

And Sine, how about you, any news from your old boyfriend?

Sine: No, *(shrugs)* I think maybe he never come to me again. Maybe I find new man to make me happy again.

Aer: We find together. One man for you and one man for me *(smiling and touching Sine's shoulder)*.

Sine: I don't think so. But I don't want to think like that. I want to think like you, and we find love.

Aer: Sorry, we must go work. Good luck to you.

Thanks, and good luck to both of you!

Sine: Thank you! I hope so.

25

FA AND EVE: "MAYBE NEXT LIFE I WILL BE FAMOUS AND RICH"

Sukhumvit Road in Bangkok begins underneath an elevated toll-way. It runs southeast through the city, and is home to two of the three major adult entertainment areas for tourists. Sitting on Sukhumvit Road, approximately one kilometre from its beginning, is an underground "coffee shop" well known to ex-pats and tourists. The girls can sit for free, they aren't required to buy a drink, as they are the draw for the drink buying customers, who come from Europe, North and South America and Asia. I met Fa and Eve at an upstairs bar, where they were getting ready to head down to "work". They had heard about the book project from a friend, who passed on word that they were interested in talking to us, in exchange for drinks while they talked. They were both in make-up and dresses you might see at a high school prom in the U.S.. Fa's was red, Eve's a dark blue. Fa has long black hair, Eve's is short and dyed a reddish brown.

Hi Fa and Eve, thanks for talking to me. You know why I want to speak with you, right?

Fa: Yes, our friends tell us you write the book about girls who work at the bar.

Eve: Yes.

Good, can you tell me where you are from and how old you are?

Fa: I am 22 year old. I come from ----, that is a small village very near to Cambodia. When I was little girl we walk and ride bicycle to village in Cambodia. Everyone very friendly. Today is different, because have a problem with temple and land. Have some soldier in my village and also in Cambodia.

Eve: Me, I am also 22 year old. I am also from Isaan, and near Cambodia, about 20 kilometre.

What about your families – do you have brothers and sisters? What do your parents do?

Eve: In my family there are me and three children more. I have three brothers, older. My family have a small restaurant, sell rice and chicken and pork, some fish.

Fa: My family have only me now. I have one brother, he was soldier before, but he go to the south of Thailand and he die.

I'm very sorry to hear that. Did he die in the fighting that is happening in the south? *(Note: in the four southern-most provinces there has been an ongoing clash between the government and groups who have been described as Muslim separatists, with bombings and shootings. Since 2004 there have been over 4,000 deaths. It is reported there are over 30,000 government troops in the area).*

Fa: He have accident. About maybe two year ago. They tell my father and mother about a bomb. My father and mother still sad too much. My mother she cry everyday for long time. We are *luk faet (twins)*. So now is only me.

Well, again, very sorry to hear that. Were you still at home when it happened or where you in Bangkok?

Fa: I am in Sa Kaeo, is town near my home. I work there on farm for melon.

And how did you come to do that?

Fa: I go there when I am 18. There is no work in my village, only to sell something to people from Cambodia. We have no tourist there. So [a] friend [of] my father tell him I can work farm and earn salary about 3,000 baht to plant and pick up the melon. So I go.

And how was the work?

Fa: Oh, very, very hard. Have to work in big field,

check the melon to see if finish, then put in bag. Work all day, have only one day off every month. I live with many worker together. *(Laughs)* I get strong, but no like too much. When my brother die I come home and then come to Bangkok for work.

And what did you do in Bangkok then?

Fa: *(looking surprised)* I do this. Work bar.

You came to Bangkok knowing you would be working like this? Were you afraid? What did you think about it?

Fa: *(shrugs her shoulders)* I think it will be better than to work on a farm. I have sex before with boys from Sa Kaeo. Only two. But every girl in Issan know about come to Bangkok or Pattaya and be bar girl. Money is good for us.

But you didn't think there was anything else you could do? Even in Bangkok, like be a maid or work in a restaurant?

Fa: *(thinks for a moment, then shrugs)* No. Why work at job like that? Can make only salary a little, same as work on farm. I have to take care my mother and father, they have no son now.

Do you think that if your brother had not died you would not be doing this?

(Fa looks at Eve and they whisper back and forth)

Fa: No, I would do this I think if my brother not

dead. This life is not so bad.

Eve, do you feel the same way, that this life is not so bad? And how did you end up working?

Eve: *(shrugs her shoulders)* Yes, this life is okay for me. I have my friend Fa, we have more friends. We do this together. I also come about two year ago. I come and work Thai massage, but work is too hard and salary is not enough.

Did you work massage here in Bangkok? And what was your salary?

Eve: Yes, I work massage in Bangkok, near to here. My salary is about 4,000 baht for month, must work everyday. Start ten o'clock in morning, finish midnight. If do massage get small tip, maybe 50 baht. Yes, was Thai massage only, no sex. I learn in massage school in Korat *(large city in northeast Thailand)*.

And now how much do you make in one month?

Fa: If have many customer come, can make 25,000 baht one month, sometime more. But in low season, no customer, maybe only 10,000 baht.

Eve: *(nodding her head)* Yes, some night have good customer, or two customer, can make 2,000 or 3,000 baht. Sometime not have customer three or four day.

So sometimes you have more than one customer in a night?

Eve: *(giving a quizzical look)* Yes, why not? We have

189

to make money.

Fa: *(nodding)* Yes, if some man want me and then another want me I can go. Because some night have no customer.

How much do you charge a customer?

Fa: For short time, about 1,500 baht. I do not go with customer for long time.

Eve: Same for short time. I will go for long time if pay me 3,000 baht.

Fa, why won't you go for the whole night?

Fa: Don't like. Customer want sex too much, or maybe in morning not want to pay or have some problem like that. Better go home in night.

And what do you think about selling sex? Does it ever make you feel bad, what you do?

Fa: *(thinks for a moment)* If the man is nice and friendly, no, no problem for me. I feel I can do for the customer and then he pay and we finish.

You mean you forget about the sex after it is over?

Fa: Yes. For me it is job. Better than work farm. Why you don't understand?

Well, many people would say you are selling yourself, that it is not a good thing to be doing.

Eve: I work massage, work very hard, I go to my room

after and my finger hurt and hand and arm, everything. I tired too much, and then go work again next time. Same everyday. Is that good? Now, I work bar I can go nine o'clock, ten o'clock at night. Have customer one hour, can go home or find more customer. Can go disco or eat with friend, relax. I don't mind this work. **Neither of you has talked about children, do you have any?**

Eve: No.

Fa: No.

Do you think about the future? About getting married, having children?

Eve: Yes, I will do this maybe two or three years more. Then I will open massage school in my village or in Korat. I have certificate. And I will give money to my parents. For me, I don't want to get married now. Maybe later. And have a family. That would make my parents happy. But now I am still young. So I can do this and then I have a new life.

Fa, what about you?

Fa: Yes, I would like to have two children, one boy and one girl. And I can take care [of] them and they will go to school and be very happy. But for husband I don't know. I want good man, but where to find? Men always butterfly, you know, playboy. And Thai man drink too much and many are no good to wife. So I don't know. Maybe can find good foreign man for husband. Can buy house and I can take care [of] him and children and house.

So Fa, how much longer do you think you will work like this?

Fa: Not sure. I am young, same [as] Eve. I want to have money for me. So I don't know. Maybe three year, five year?

What do you think about the customers? Do you like any of them? Would you marry one or have one for a boyfriend if they asked you not to work?

Eve: Marry customer? I don't think so, but I know some girl have foreign husband, so maybe. I don't think about that. Customer is customer. You see the person work 7-Eleven shop? What they think about the customer there? Nothing. I think the same [as] them.

Fa: If the customer is friendly and happy, I like to go with them. They make me laugh, buy drink, I think they are good person. Yes, if some man tell me "now you don't work like this, I give you money for family and room and food," sure, okay, I stop for him. But who do that? I know some girl stop for man maybe one month, two month, then man don't want no more. Girl have broken heart, and *seea nah (lose face)*, have to come back bar, everybody say "Oh, what happen you boyfriend?" It okay if have gold or can show money in bank, but if cannot, then no good for girl. But if I can find a good man with good heart who want to take care [of] me, okay I can stay with him.

What about when you have sex with customers, do you worry about HIV, do you always use a condom?

Fa: Yes, always or no sex. I will not do sex without condom. I not want to be sick and die. No money, no honey *(laughing)*. But no condom, no sex.

Eve: I am same. Sometime lady not use condom, have some problem, or get pregnant. I don't want.

Well, that's good to hear. Anything else you want to say? What do you think about a book about you and your friends, your lives? Both of you seem like you don't think that this life is hard.

Eve: Sometime I am lonely, I know my family not know what I do. This life is not so easy, but it is not so hard like before and for some other girl I know in my village. So my life is okay, I like some thing, I don't like some thing. Maybe next life I will be famous and rich, and have very good life. *(Laughs)*

Fa: Book is English book? The book good for foreign man. They can know about Thai lady. Some guy should be careful. We know about man come here, drink too much, give lady money too much, want to marry, have a big problem. Maybe this man can find me and give me money *(laughing)*. We want man to be happy, but we want to be happy, too.

26

DTO AND DAK: "I DREAM A GOOD MAN WILL WANT TO MARRY ME"

Dto and Dak are Vietnamese women who work the nightclubs and bars of Phnom Penh, Cambodia. They worked their way out of the infamous K-11 brothels, and now live together in Phnom Penh.

Q: Hello Dak and Dto. Thank you for talking with me. I just want to find out about your lives and what you think about your work. Please tell me about yourselves – how old are you, where do you come from?

Dto: I am 24 years old. I come from Vietnam. My mama and poppa, they live in Vietnam, near the border with Cambodia. They stay in a village there with many other families. The village [is] very poor. That is where we come from. Everyone there try to be a farmer but sometime it is not so good and very hard to make enough money for everyone to eat. So my friend Dak and me, we came to Phnom Penh to live and earn money to send home to our families.

Dak: I come here to Phnom Penh with my friend Dak about almost three years ago. Now I am 20 years old. My family live in Vietnam. They also are very poor. I have no father. I have my mother, two sister and two brother.

Did your families want you to come here?

Dto: My mother cry when we leave. My father not home when we leave. He working. But is better to help my family. They have not enough to eat and my parents are old.

Dak: My family cry too. My sister are young. They do not understand why I have to go.

Did your families know what you came here to do, how you would earn your money?

Dak: Yes, my mother know. But not my sister or brother. Sometimes I am scared and feel alone, but I know this what is best for me, to send money home to my father and my brothers. My father die about eight year ago. He riding on the motorcycle, and have accident with bus. I was in school. It was very hard for family. We all very sad. I have to leave school and work in small shop, clean fish, but I cannot make enough money for family. I miss my father very much. Sometime I think if he did not die, he would not have let his daughter have life like I have. But now I can only do what I know is best for my family.

Dto: Yes, my mother know, and my father. My mother talk to me, tell me to not be afraid. What I will do I will do so my family can have a better life. Then I can come back someday and it will be okay. My father he does not talk to me before I leave.

What were your lives like in Vietnam? You say you were poor – did you go to school? Did you have enough to eat?

Dak: My house at home has one room for everyone. Toilet is outside. When I was little girl we don't have light, but now we do. But we are poor – have food but nothing more. One bicycle. Motorcycle? No, not after my father die. Always wear old clothes, when I was little I don't have shoe. I go to school sometimes, but have to work more.

Dto: I have nothing. I try to go to Ho Chi Minh City to work, but many people try to work there, and it dangerous. I don't learn so much in school. I can read and write, but our school never have computer.

Okay, I am asking this because it might be hard for people who don't know to understand how working here – selling your body – is better than being poor on the farm in Vietnam, or working in a restaurant in Ho Chi Minh City.

Dto: If I work farm my life will never be better. If I

work in restaurant it is a very hard life. And still work for little money.

Dak: Yes, we cannot get job in city, we are country girl – people treat us bad.

But if you could, would you leave this life here in Cambodia?

Dak: I want to go home every day, but we must do what we must do.

Dto: I pray that will happen – to leave this place.

What can you tell us about your lives now?

Dto: Now I live in a room not too far from here, with my friend Dak. It is small room; we have only one bed, we sleep together. Sometime it is noisy, because some other people in the house get drunk. And there are also many dogs around. For our room we pay $2 every day. I have to send money home to my mama and papa. When we come to Cambodia first time, we work in house *(K-11)* because we have friends [there] who came to Phnom Penh to work. Our friends in Phnom Penh met many men from Japan and America and Europe and send money home and help their family. Sure we know what the job is to be, but we want to come so our families can eat. We come three years ago. First we have to work in the house, because the *mamasan* let us live there and earn money. But sometime it was very bad. At first I did not like it and cry all the time with Dak. We had to have sex with any man who come to the house. If he like the girl, the girl cannot say no. Sometime they not give girl tip, sometime girl get $1 or $5. Sometime I had to go with three or four or five men one day. We stay there for more than one year. But then we pay [the] *mamasan* and now we live here, and go to some bars in town. I like to meet the men, some are very nice, but I have problem because I can only speak a little English and they cannot speak Vietnamese. But now we try to go with men we like. Sometime if I need money I will go with men I do not like, even if they are drunk, but I try not to do that. Sometimes they get mad because they cannot make love.

So are you sad about your life?

Dak: Sometimes sad. Many Khmer *(Cambodian)* girls here do not like us because men like the Vietnam girl more. They say we are more beautiful. So I am sad because we have not too many friends sometimes.

Dto: I am not sad. I know I will have a happy life someday. Maybe sometime I will meet a man who has a big house in America and he will marry me. I look at books and movies about America and think I would like to live there. I think I can make good wife for a man in America. I would like a man who can take care of me and send money to my family. I want to have children, maybe many if my husband is a good man. I want to learn about computers and then I can get a good job to take care of my children and father and mother.

What do you think about the men you meet?

Dto: I like to meet men at the discos. When they are nice and buy me drinks and dance with me. Sometime I like to make love, but not if the man tells me to go home when he finish. Sometime I go with a man to beautiful room at hotel and want to stay, be in big bed and watch TV.

Dak: Many men are nice, many are not so nice. Now I try to know the man before I go with him.

Have either of you had a customer be your boyfriend?

Dto: I do not have a boyfriend. Before, I met a man who stay about three weeks and I stay with him. He say he will find me when he come back. Some very nice men I remember. I have one man from Europe who wrote me a letter once, but I could not understand it, I hope he said he remember me and love me. I want to see him again if he come back to Cambodia.

Dak: No, I waiting *(laughs)*. Maybe sometime I will have a boyfriend, and a husband, but now I have no one like that.

Do you ever get to go home and see your families?

Dak: No. I have not seen my family now for three years. They write me a letter sometime, and sometime some friend bring a picture to me.

Dto: Same as my friend. I never go to see them. I will see them when I go home to live.

Do you get lonely, miss your families?

Dak: I think we get lonely and miss our families very much. But we cannot go home because they are too poor and we have to help them by working here.

Dto: I miss my family. Everyday. But I know what I must do. Later I want to buy a house for my parents and live in the country with them.

So even though you have to work like you do, is it better here or in Vietnam?

Dto: Yes, it is better here than Vietnam. Here I can make $40 or $50 in one night, sometimes more if I have some good luck. The man I stayed with for three week, he pay me more than $500! I did not have to go out to work. He buy me food, clothes, he let Dak come with us to eat and shop.

What about the future – how long do you think you will be here?

Dak: I want to go back soon, but I do not know. When I go back, maybe with a husband. I want to have two children with good father. In maybe one or two years that is what I want.

We are talking to you so we can write what you say in a book. What do you want to say about your life to people who will read the book?

Dto: I like to talk about my life for the book; maybe a good man will read about me and want to marry me (*smiling*).

Dak: I think it is a good thing if many people learn about what my life is like. Sometime my life is good, and I am happy. Sometimes it is not good, but what can I do. This is my life here.

27

ED, THE BAR OWNER: "DON'T MISTAKE YOUR FUN FOR REALITY"

The city of Pattaya is located on the Gulf of Thailand approximately 150 kilometres southeast of Bangkok. It is estimated that in high season (November through April) Pattaya's population peaks at around 105,000 Thai and foreign residents, with that number dropping to as low as 70,000 during the low season, as tourists and Thai workers head home.

In April 1961 the first of what would eventually be thousands of American servicemen landed in the town for a bit of rest and relaxation before shipping off to Vietnam. Pattaya changed from a small fishing village to one of the most famous getaways on the planet.

"Ed" is the owner of a beer bar in Pattaya. He first came to Pattaya in 1965 and has lived there since 1985. He provided me with his insights on the city and ownership of a bar in Thailand.

Q: Ed, thanks for meeting with me. You're a bar owner here; there seems to be no shortage of foreigners willing

to invest in the bar scene. What's your feeling on that?

Ed: In one word? Don't. We have a saying here: the surest way to end up with a million dollars in Thailand is to start with three. I ended up with this place by accident. I suppose it's all been worthwhile, but there's easier ways to make a living, for sure.

Do you want to explain "the accident" that got you into this?

It's a long story, it involves several decades.

That's no problem. Can you start with your introduction to Thailand?

Yeah, that's way back. I was an 18 year old gung-ho U.S. Marine. I had wanted to leave home in Texas and joining the marines was a sure way to do that. We were training the South Vietnamese Army, mostly in crowd control, but in other things too, and they *(the U.S. Army)* had been flying guys over to Thailand for a couple of years for "R&R". Then I guess someone got the idea to truck the guys from the air bases out in the country, down to the beach. A little town called Pattaya. My first trip was from Bangkok in the back of a big green truck; there were probably eight or 12 of us bouncing around, trying to drink cans of beer. We couldn't see the road, but it couldn't have been paved. It took three hours *(note: that same trip today takes an hour and a half*). When we got out and looked around we said "What the hell?" There was nothing but a couple of green huts on the beach. The streets were dirt paths, there were no streetlights. You could see stars and hear the waves washing up on shore. I remember that. It reminded me of a desert island. But there were girls waiting for us. Literally lined up. Country girls down to make money. We were just dropped off and they told us "See you in five days". There were no MP's to watch over us like today. There was nothing to do though. Well, sit on the beach, drink and have sex with the girls. The USO *(United Service Organization)* or someone tried to put together a couple of cultural shows – singing and dancing, but there wasn't much interest *(laughing)*. We got around by hiring what were called *samlors* – bicycles; well, tricycles really, and two people could sit on the back while an old Thai guy pedaled away.

You said the girls were lined up, what was their attitude towards you? We've heard that the reason guys preferred R&R in Thailand to Hong Kong was that the women were friendlier.

Oh yeah. The women in Hong Kong were notorious for being expensive and cold. You knew they only wanted money, and as much as they could get. Pretty much the same in Vietnam, and of course the Catholics had been into Vietnam and told them all they'd burn in hell for having sex. But Thailand was different. They had that Thai *sanook (fun)* attitude. Thais in general had a very relaxed attitude towards sex – more puritan views came in, I think anyway, as a reaction to what happened.

And what happened?

Well, as soon as word got out that girls were making 500 baht a night, there were bus-loads of girls arriving from the provinces. Some Thai entrepreneurs opened up beer bars, then go-go bars and then the sex shows.

Wasn't that going on in Bangkok? What was the scene there?

Not in the beginning. Soi Cowboy *(a street full of go-go and beer bars in downtown Bangkok)* only had one or two bars on it. The first one was opened by a black guy from Houston, he was retired Air Force – "Cowboy" – that's who the street is named after. There was the Lone Star Bar across and down the road, which was a big hang-out for, well, let's just say guys who were into "classified" stuff. If you weren't recognized no one would say much to you. But as the numbers of Americans grew, so did the bar scene. Chiang Mai *(the largest city in northern Thailand)* was a village, it had only one bar, the Blue Moon. That's long gone now.

Were there a lot of Americans in Bangkok at that time?

Unless you were around the embassy or JUSMAG *(military headquarters)* you stood out. By '68 and '69 things had picked up. There were an incredible number of people behind the scenes of the war. Do you know that for every grunt on the front lines there were something like 20 people sitting in offices connected with the war? And a whole lot of them were in Thailand. "REMFs" we called them "Rear Echelon Mother Fuckers".

So you saw the whole scene grow?

Yeah, but the feeling was very different. It wasn't a bunch of folks on holiday. We were into some serious business in Vietnam and this was a place to come and get rid of a load of pressure, so it was fun, yeah, but it wasn't exactly what you think of as a holiday. But by '72 I had gone back to the states. I came in and out over the next few years, but only on short assignments. I did manage to meet my wife on one of those assignments though. By '84 I'd put my 20 years in, I was stationed in Hawaii, and it just seemed like the right time to retire. Only thing was I wasn't sure what the hell to do. Then a buddy of mine said, "Let's buy a little hotel in Thailand, rent out a few rooms and live for free." Now I knew it wasn't going to be that easy, but I figured, "What the hell," so we went 50/50 on this small guest house. Six months later my buddy goes home to Easton, Pennsylvania – where the fighter Larry Holmes is from – gets religion, and tells me keep the whole thing, he's done with a life of sin. So, here I am. I put in a little restaurant, catered mostly to service related people. I did pretty well, there was no bar attached, but as time went on it became apparent that I'd have to have a bit more to draw in the customers, that's just the way it was. So my wife – we've been together on and off, mostly on, for 30 years – put out the word that we were looking for a few "hostesses" and I had more applying than I knew what to do with. Just like in the beginning with the guest house it was mostly customers we knew, but as time goes on, you know, things change. It became a business, a break-even business. You can't live on what the bar takes in. If you're any kind of a person you have to pay the girls a decent salary. What do I pay them? More than most, let's say. Anyone abroad would probably be shocked, but it's a decent wage for the girls here. And they get 50 baht for every drink bought for them and half the bar fine if they want to go with a customer.

Do the girls have a choice in whether to go with a customer or not?

Oh yeah, we wouldn't force anyone to do anything. The bar fine is 500 baht before midnight, 300 after.

Whatever the girls work out with their friend is up to them. What do they get? I would guess most of them between 1,500 – 2,000 baht for all night.

Do you require the girls to get medical check-ups for HIV and STDs?

Yes. No exceptions. Every month. I pay for it, too. And we give the girls condoms. It's for the protection of them and the customer.

So what's not to love about the business?

HA! Where to start? There's payoffs. To who? Who do you think? Do you know that for police officers, being assigned here is one of the most sought after posts? They have to buy their assignment here. And they make that back through collecting, shall we say, dues. For what? Liquor license, check to make sure you don't have unlicensed music on your system, not open too late or serving liquor on holidays. They might stop by every so often just to say hello, make sure everything is okay. If I'm lucky I can get off handing out a bottle of whiskey. There's always something. Then you've got the girls. We try to be careful about who we hire – no druggies, nobody who gets out of hand drunk. But it happens. And the girls will fight at the drop of a hat. We had a little jackpot between our girls and the ones from down the street. They said our girls were talking bad about their bar. Turns out it was customers doing the talking, but we had two full blown fist-fights out in the street here in a week. No one wanted to get in the middle of it. One even had the cops come by. Two of them on a scooter. They looked at what was going on, it was three or four girls going at it, and the cops just drove slowly around them and kept on going down the street, didn't even get off the scooter. And you've watched the Thai soap operas? Seems like the girls need their lives to be just as dramatic, if not more, than what's on television. Don't get me wrong, most of them have good hearts, but many of them aren't well educated. A rumour starts and it's impossible to convince them it might not be true. Like what? You can or can't get HIV from doing this or that. Last year it was a ghost was dragging girls into the water at the beach south of here. So there's that. There's dealing with the customers – they fall in love, or what they think is love with the girls. You can share your experiences with them, but they insist, "This one is different." There are so many problems – most of these girls are, like I said, not very worldly. Their life experience is a village in the north or northeast of Thailand and the bars of Pattaya or Bangkok. Many of them have been abused as kids, taken out of school at eight, nine or ten years old. Their

English is limited. I tell them "Take her to a buffet at one of these big hotels, see how it goes." They won't eat food they aren't familiar with. Give them a choice of spicy papaya salad and a fillet and they'll go for the good old Som Tom every time. If the temperature here drops to 60 degrees *(Fahrenheit)* they put on hats and gloves and sweaters. You're going to bring a girl like that to Chicago or Sweden? Good luck. But they think you're trying to break them apart, keep the girl at the bar. Man, I'm trying to save them both from a lot of grief.

I've talked to a few girls who have gone through that – going abroad and then learning they miss Thailand and their families.

Right, and the families. When you hook up with one of these girls, you're getting the whole family in the deal. Mother, father, siblings, grandma and grandpa. And their kids, if they have them. Some of them still have husbands back in the village. The girls are under tremendous pressure to support the family, and believe me, the family will always come first. Let's say a couple have a house or condo here in town. The family will come for a visit. Some of them will go home in a week or two, but then the guy finds there's a brother or cousin who stayed behind and suddenly has a job down the street. What are you going to do, throw the kid out? You can't. The girl will lose face. And there's been more than once when the poor guy finds out the cousin isn't a cousin – he's the husband from the village. So can you trust any of them? It's the same with any profession, right? Lawyers, salesmen, whatever. Some are honest, some just aren't. The last thing I'll say about that is, if you do get involved, make sure you are worth more alive than dead. Do a little internet search. More than a few *farang* husbands have ended up dead in fairly mysterious circumstances. Their big mistake? "Yes honey, don't worry. If anything happens to me, you get the house and pick-up truck and X amount of baht." I guess this all sounds pretty depressing, but it's the realistic side of things. Are there "happily ever after" couples out there? Probably. But there's far more tales of woe.

What about you and your wife – you said you'd been together 30 years. Any words of wisdom from your own experience?

I knew when we got together I was in it for the long haul. She, and I know you hear this all the time, but I swear its true; and you know what's coming, right? She was not a bar girl. She was in teacher's college, her family is from Chonburi, just up the road. I was respectable,

212

too. She finished college, taught elementary school, then when I ended up with the place on my own she asked if she could help. I couldn't have done it without her, as it turns out. Anyways, her parents weren't thrilled, but I had been an officer and I was impressive in my uniform. Her father's friends were impressed, anyway. So that won him over in the beginning. And later on I said, "Don't worry I will always make sure she is taken care of." That's really what he wanted to hear. Not "I'll make her happy, I'll never cheat on her, I'll love her each and every hour of every day." He wanted to hear "I'll take care of her". See, at least to her generation and before, that's what "love" is all about. I don't know what they're thinking today, maybe western movies and Thai television have changed things, but for many years here love has been about providing. Probably about what it was like in the states in the 1800's. So you have to learn to adapt. There's books written about this culture stuff. When they say it's difficult, it's nothing to laugh at. Be patient, be cool. Thais don't respond well to public displays of anger. Do not, do not, make someone "lose face" – lose respect, especially in front of others. Don't expect them to plan a lot of things out carefully in advance. It's pay as you go. If you're good at taking things in your stride, you're fine. If you're not, stay in

New York or Frankfurt or wherever.

That's a big part of why I'm talking to you. There is the realistic side that people don't or won't see. You said your wife comes from a nice family, who are not in the bar business, and now she helps you out. Isn't that unusual? Don't most "good families" want nothing to do with the business?

Well, that has a lot to do with the on and off of the relationship. At first she left when we talked about adding a bar. But then she thought she'd be better off being a partner and keeping an eye on me than walking away from it all. Thais know this place *(Pattaya)* exists. Hell, as big as the scene in Pattaya is, it's nothing compared to the business that caters to the Thais and Chinese, and the Koreans and Japanese. You go out in parts of Bangkok and you'll think you've wandered into Las Vegas it's so lit up. All big massage parlours; 400, 500 girls. And if you ain't Asian, chances are you ain't getting in. So in answer to your question, she thinks it's better if she takes care of the girls and keeps tabs on me and the bar.

Back to the bar – what's the economic reality?

Ah, the money *(laughing)*. I break even. Maybe make a little during high season, but run at a loss in low season. I try not to lay any of the girls off. Some of [them] go home for the Songkran holiday *(Thai New Year in mid-April)* and don't come back until October. But if I didn't have the pension coming in, I'd be broke. Truth is I've been trying to sell the place for awhile, but apparently there aren't that many people out there wanting to start a new lucrative life *(laughing)*. Actually I get a few calls, but maybe I'm too honest about what's involved. I don't want anyone getting into something they have no idea about.

I'll tell you a story; it didn't happen here, happened in a town on the other side of the gulf, but someone here ended up with the bar. Young kid from England bought a small place – just a bar and a few tables, nothing fancy. Paid a million baht upfront for the rent, license, the liquor, chairs, tables. Opened up, put in a small sound system. Police come by. "Music fee" is 30,000 baht. He had bought a TV and a few DVD's. They pulled the DVD's – copies. 20,000 baht "fine". He couldn't get beer or liquor or even soda on credit. His wife hired the girls, but she had no experience, so the girls were a disaster. Got drunk, got advances on their salaries and never came back. It took just under a year, know what he sold for? 100,000 baht. I heard he bought a ticket back home with the money. That's what you don't want to happen.

So what is your personal feeling about the girls, their lives – do you feel sorry for them?

Huh. I guess in a way I do. Very few do this out of really free choice. Like I said, there's a lot of pressure to support the family. They come from poverty most westerners can't imagine. There's very little hope of going to high school or university, of getting a decent job. Work in a leather factory or a bar. There's more money in the bar job, and in the end, who's to say which is better for them?

So what's the answer?

For the whole deal? There isn't one. This, prostitution in Thailand, was going on long before we white folks arrived. And if we all disappeared tomorrow it would go on some more. But for individual girls? Sure, education, if you could find some way to pay for it. They may not be worldly, but they aren't stupid by any means. But then you'd have to get them to go. Send them to a computer or English or beauty school, if they could be motivated they'd do well. But then you've got some that like what they do, hard as that might be for folks to take in.

Do you ever feel like what you are doing isn't quite, ah, respectable?

Yeah, I guess if I told folks back in Cleveland, [or] Texas, "Hey, I run a bar in Thailand where you can buy a girl for an hour or a night," well, it doesn't sound too nice does it? But this is a different world here, different values. So no, in the circumstance of life here, I'm good with it. Unless of course someone makes me a decent offer. Then I'd be done with it.

All right, thanks for your time and insight, Ed, anything else you'd like to add?

You know, a lot of these girls have gotten a bad deal in life and are just trying to make it better for them and their families. You can have some fun, a lot of fun. I will say this, treat the girls decent and chances are they'll do the same. But don't mistake your fun for reality. And always remember, they got more experience at this game than you do.

GLOSSARY

(*= Thai word in English)

Ab Nuat*: "Bath massage". A massage parlor where the massage includes a bath or shower with the masseuse. They are not the same as "Thai Massage" which are legitimate massage businesses and do not offer sex.

Baht*: Thai currency. Approximately 30 baht to 1 USD; 48 baht to one British Pound; 41 baht to one Euro.

Bar beer: Also called "beer bar". An indoor or outdoor bar which, of course, sells beer. Usually, but not always, the main attraction of a "bar beer" is the availability of working girls.

Bar fine: An amount that the customer must pay the bar in order to take a worker, waitress or dancer outside. It can vary from 100 baht to 800 baht or more, depending on the bar and time of day or night, and whether for a short time or long time. The term usually used by the women is to ask the customer to "pay bar".

Butterfly: A playboy, someone who has many women in their life.

Chiang Mai: The largest city in Northern Thailand.

Chock wow*: Thai for masturbate (males); the term for women is "took baet".

Farang*: The Thai word for "foreigner", it is generally used now to refer to western foreigners.

Go-hok*: A lie or a liar.

Isaan*: The northeast area of Thailand. The area is a rural farming area, and is the poorest area in Thailand. The majority of bar girls come from Isaan.

Kee-nee-ow*: A person who is cheap, a cheapskate.

Long time: When a woman goes with a customer overnight.

Mamasan: The female manager of a bar. Her duties include everything from scheduling and paying to counseling the women and handling customers. Many of the women call the mamasan "Maeh", the Thai word for "mother".

Nong Kai: A fairly large town in northern Thailand, on the border with Laos.

Patpong: An area of Bangkok famous for its go-go bars and sex shows, it has now been reduced to a very few bars, almost no shows and a few discos. The draw now are stalls which sell copies of designer watches, jeans, bags, etc.

Pattaya: A city approximately 150 kilometers southeast of Bangkok. It has been called the "world's biggest brothel" and the number of working women has been estimated at anywhere from 5,000 to 10,000 (out of a population which has been estimated at between 75,000-100,000, depending on the area defined as "Pattaya proper"). For example, Jomtien is a small enclave south of Pattaya, but usually included when referring to Pattaya. There has been an effort to clean up the image of Pattaya since 2005, although still if you mention you are going to Pattaya you will get a knowing nod and a wink.

Pew cow*: Literally "white skin". In Thailand, as in much of Asia, white skin is desirable, darker skin is a sign of "farmers"; for which the Thai word is "pew dahm". Skin color is a dividing line between the classes in Thailand.

Phuket: A province in southern Thailand that is an island, although connected to the mainland by bridge. It is a popular tourist destination and has a sizeable bar scene.

Soi Cowboy: A one block stretch of go-go and beer bars in Bangkok.

Som Tom*: Papaya salad. Very popular with people from Isaan.

Short time: When a woman goes with a customer only for sex.

Tee-lok* (or Tee-rok): Sweetheart, lover.

Yaba*: Literally "crazy drug". It is methamphetamine sold in pill form. Manufactured in clandestine laboratories in Burma, it is widely used by Thais.